'HOW TO'

BOOK OF
HERBS AND
HERB
GARDENING

ANN BONAR

BROCKHAMPTON PRESS

The 'HOW TO' Book of Herbs
and Herb Gardening has been
written and designed to explain,
in the most concise way, how
to grow herbs for their culinary,
decorative and medicinal values,
how to design and plan a
herb garden, and how to
use the herbs you grow.

'HOW TO'

Contents

The 'How To' Book of Herbs and Herb
Gardening was conceived, edited and
designed by Simon Jennings and Company Limited,
42 Maiden Lane, London WC2, England

This edition published 1996 by
Brockhampton Press Ltd,
20 Bloomsbury Street,
London WC1B 3QA

Text and illustrations
© 1981 Simon Jennings & Co Ltd

ISBN 1 86019 249 1

Printed and bound in U.A.E.

THE AUTHOR
Ann Bonar is a gardening
writer, journalist, and
practising gardener. Her
career has included
advisory work for fruit
farmers, garden
consultancy, lecturing in
horticulture and five years
editing gardening books.
Plant hunting in many
European countries has
given her a considerable
knowledge of herbs, and
she is the author of several
books on this and other
gardening subjects. Her
titles in the 'How To' series
include: *Basic Gardening,
Vegetable Gardening* and
Flower Gardening.

Introduction

Gardening is not immune to the current interest in antiques, antiquities and the past generally. The revival of enthusiasm for herbs and their cultivation is partly because of their historical associations which stretch back to beyond neolithic times.

Some of their fascination is due to the myths and legends which have collected round them. For example, the mandrake *(Mandragora officinalis)* is said to shriek and groan when dug up, and any who hear it die at once. The literature surrounding herbs is extensive, and much of it comes from mediaeval herbals, some of which are still available in modern reprintings.

But the present popularity of herbs is also due to the rediscovery that their flavours can lift a recipe out of the good, into the top class. They put new life and taste into food, much of which, nowadays, has lost its piquancy – adding salt often simply makes it taste salty instead of enhancing the natural flavour. Additionally, some of them have appreciable food value, for example, Vitamin C in parsley, and iron in sorrel.

The 'back-to-nature' trend, too, has resulted in experimenting with the use of herbs for cosmetics. Not only are they included in proprietary shampoos, astringents and after-shave lotions, but recipes for making them up at home can be found in magazines, books and newspaper articles.

Herbs are easily grown and, unlike many plants, they are hardly afflicted with pests and diseases. It has been said that this immunity to ailments is the reason for their efficacy in curing human and animal ailments. Whether this is true or not, the spiralling cost of laboratory-made drugs, together with their side-effects and decreasing usefulness, has brought about renewed interest in the medical usefulness of herbs.

Whatever your leaning, there is always a place for a herb collection somewhere in the garden. Many are ornamental and grow happily in a border, but they probably show to their best advantage in a formal design, especially one similar to an Elizabethan knot garden.

Angelica

Chives

Culinary herbs
Herbs had been used for centuries to improve and mask the flavour of poor quality and bad meat before they became an essential part of *haute cuisine,* Chives, parsley and mint, *above,* are among the most commonly used. Angelica, *top left,* is usually candied and used for cake decoration.

What is a herb?

The botanical definition of a herb is that it is a plant with no persistent stem above ground. However, since the group of plants now considered to be herbs includes the shrub rosemary and the tree sweet bay, such a definition is not appropriate. For all practical purposes, herbs are those plants with aromatic or perfumed parts, whether they are leaves, stems, roots, flowers or fruits, which are used in cooking, medicine or cosmetics.

Many plants were grown as herbs, mainly for medicinal use, but some also for use in cooking, that are no longer regarded as herbs. Marigolds, roses and violets are now grown as treasured inhabitants of the ornamental garden, but were once part of every apothecary's store.

A conserve made of the flowers of marigolds and sugar was said by Gerard in his Herbal (1597) to 'cure the trembling of the heart'. *Rosa damascena* (the Damask Rose) appears to have been able to cure practically anything, judging from Culpeper's *Complete Herbal* published in the middle of the 17th century, and violets were used to provide an antiseptic (the leaves) and a laxative (the flowers and roots).

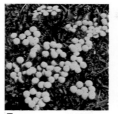
Tansy

Marigold

Medicinal herbs
Most plants have been tried at some time, in the hope that they will effect remedies for a vast assortment of ailments. Many of those whose reputation survives are still used in medicine. Comfrey, *above*, is one which has proven healing properties – as well as being a remarkably effective compost making agent.

Ornamental herbs
There are many herbs which have attractive flowers and foliage as well as their practical uses, and many border plants which possess herbal properties. Tansy and marigolds, *top*, provide striking colour in the herbaceous border. Foxgloves (*Digitalis purpurea*), above, although poisonous, are common in many gardens.

7

Herbs in history

It is probably because herbs have been used for so many thousands of years that they have collected a mass of legends, stories and magical poetry round them, and have been associated with witchcraft and spells. To some extent, this is the fault of those using them medicinally. Some cures must have appeared miraculous to the victim though the explanation, once known, was simple. But faith played a large part in curing, and a certain amount of 'mumbo-jumbo' helped to bring results.

Borage acquired a reputation among the Greeks and Romans for being a bringer of courage; perhaps the courage was Dutch, since the herb was

put into wines and wine-cups. Sage was once regarded as a cure for every ill under the sun, and an Arabic proverb says: 'How can a man die who has sage in his garden?'

Parsley seed was supposed to be a cure for baldness, and if seed was taken before drinking alcohol, it would 'helpeth men that have weyke braynes to beare drinks better'. Angelica mostly comes into flower around 8th May, St Michael the Archangel's day, and the root was often used in rituals against witches and spells.

The first herbalists

The first use that plants had for man was as food. The cave-dwellers discovered by trial and error, sometimes fatal, what was good to eat and what was not. Later, plants provided fibres for clothing, and dyes for that clothing. Someone, more observant than most, must have noticed that wounds or injuries accidentally painted with the blue dye obtained from woad healed much more quickly than the others.

Gradually, a list of plants accumulated which would alleviate or cure sickness and injury, and those people with specialist knowledge of these plants became herbalists or apothecaries. In Europe, first the Romans, then the Druids, and later the monks of the monastic orders, provided the doctors of the community; all had a special garden in which to grow the herbs they needed.

In time, plants began to be cultivated for ornament, as well as for medicine and food, and much experimenting with flavours became fashionable. By the mid 16th Century no housewife worth her salt could have a herb garden with less than 50 different culinary herbs in it.

Until the early part of the 17th Century, herbs were an essential part of everyday life and provided cordials, tisanes and teas, flavourings, perfumes, cosmetics, medicines and salads. The most famous herbals come from this time, including Turner's Herbal, *circa* 1556.

William Turner is known as the Father of English botany, and he was the first to detail the places in which herbs could be found growing wild. Gerard's Herbal, 1597, is another which has come down to us; the author became the Master of the Worshipful Company of Apothecaries in 1607.

Culpeper's Herbal, produced sometime during the 1640s, was the last of the great herbals, and it was about this time that plant hunting and discovery got going in earnest. The flood of new ornamental plants that came into the country, together with the fashionable trend towards elegantly designed gardens, swamped the herbs, especially as new medicines and new medical treatments were being discovered.

Nevertheless, the use of herbs did not die completely, and interest in them, although diminished, remained sufficiently alive to take on a new lease of life during the twentieth century. This revival shows no sign of waning, and indeed increases yearly, particularly on the medicinal side.

Herb gardens in history

In very early times, no distinction could have been made between the garden and the *herb* garden. They were one and the same. Gardens were purely functional and the plants in them were there to provide medicines or food. The Romans and the early monastic orders showed a tendency to separate the ornamental from the functional. In Persia and India, during the 5th and 6th Centuries, rulers and rich men had well-ordered gardens composed of scented and ornamental herbs, but there was no general movement towards 'designed' herb gardens until medieval times. This was when the knot garden began to be fashionable. These gardens were laid out in fairly elaborate patterns with low-growing plants forming the lines or structure of the pattern and coloured earth or stones filling in the gaps. They were to remain in fashion until the 17th Century, when the rapid increase in botanical discovery led to an entirely new kind of ornamental garden and herbs were relegated to the kitchen garden. Since then, the interest in herb gardens has been largely academic or historical – until very recently, when the herb revival began.

Traditional formality *top left*
This bedding scheme, using flowering plants and box hedges was used in many herb gardens.

Relaxed formality *bottom left*
The herb garden at Sissinghurst, works as a kitchen garden as well as an ornamental arrangement.

Medieval herb gardens *above*
These were, invariably, a symmetrical arrangement of small beds making cultivation easier.

11

Making a choice

The cultivation of herbs can be endlessly fascinating, and can lead to all sorts of other diversions, as you get to know more about their care, and learn something of their history. Any article or book about herbs will recount yet another legend or story connected with individual kinds – some of them very far-fetched indeed.

If you are considering growing herbs, it will probably be mainly the culinary kinds, but with the modern interest in natural remedies for illnesses and injuries, you may also want to make a collection of medicinal sorts, such as aconitum, elecampane, betony and belladonna.

There are a great number of herbs for flavouring food, not just the big five of parsley, mint, thyme, chives and bay. It is very well worth expanding this number to a collection of about twenty which should at least include tarragon, rosemary, basil and fennel.

It is still quite practical, using the appropriate herbs, to make teas and tisanes to help with digestion and insomnia. Some herbs have a soothing and calming effect, others help to cleanse the blood, and yet others can be made up into eye lotions, skin tonics

Aconitum

Elecampane

Betony

and shampoos. Some are grown commercially, even now, to provide medicinal drugs for serious illnesses, but if you are contemplating home medication which involves the use of herbs, do obtain spécialist advice first as to which herbs to grow and how to use them.

Other specialist collections may include Biblical herbs, such as clary, flax, and lily; or one of the fragrant and aromatic herbs and beeplants – lavender, woodruff, rose and bergamot.

You could design an exact replica of a knot garden from an old plan, and plant a collection familiar to Elizabethans, or fill the beds with herbs mentioned in Shakespeare's plays.

Another interesting specialization is collecting the herbs of various plant families and planting them in natural order beds. The *Labiatae,* the *Umbelliferae* and the *Compositae* are three families which provide many herbs.

A nice simple collection could consist of herbs which are highly ornamental, as well as having some herbal property. There are all sorts of herbs in this category, marigolds, nasturtiums, roses, lavender, yellow gentian and catmint are a few, and you will find there are many more.

INFUSIONS FOR COSMETICS

There is a long tradition of using herbs in cosmetics – these are just a few ideas you can try at home.

Steam facial
Many herbs are suitable for this, including the flowers of elder, lime and yarrow, also the leaves of comfrey, nettle and sage. Use about 13g (½oz) of herbs in 1 litre (1¾ pints) boiling water.

Facial

Eye lotions
Most of the healing herbs can be used for eye lotions, but there seems to be more substance behind the claims for eyebright, plantain and cornflower. Use a tepid infusion.

Eye bath

Skin toners
A pack made from carrots and lemon juice is very effective, while lotions can be made from lime flowers, mallow, marigolds, lemon balm, yarrow, fennel and many others. A simple infusion will suffice for a skin lotion.

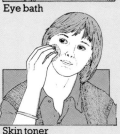
Skin toner

Culinary herbs

If you have never grown herbs, it may be best to start with some of the most easily grown, for example, mint, chives, parsley and thyme. All will grow in an ordinary garden soil and only thyme needs a sunny place. Of the other common culinary herbs, chervil, dill and marjoram are scarcely more difficult to grow, and tarragon will do well in poor soil. Bay, basil and rosemary can present some problems, especially in cool, exposed sites. But a little care and protection is usually all that is needed. When planning your garden, remember that proximity to the kitchen is important. Herbs are at their best when very fresh – so the garden should be arranged to facilitate last-minute collection.

15

Some popular culinary herbs

1	Tarragon
2	Parsley
3	Marjoram
4	Chervil
5	Sage *detail*
6	Sage *plant*
7	Thyme *detail*
8	Thyme *plant*
9	Mint
10	Rosemary *detail*
11	Rosemary *plant*
12	Bay
13	Bay *detail*
14	Chives

Apple mint in sunken pot

Keeping herbs under control

Many herbs are invasive and will quickly spread through the garden. They can be checked by sowing or planting them in sunken containers.

Herbs for flavouring

A good nucleus of herbs for flavouring would contain parsley, thyme, mint, sage and chives. A classic *bouquet garni* consists of parsley, thyme, marjoram and a bay leaf, so pot or wild marjoram, and a sweet bay in a tub would be needed as well. Bay will grow into a tree 6m (20ft) tall, but can be kept in a container, if it is regularly clipped.

Other very useful kitchen garden herbs are basil, tarragon, fennel and rosemary. All four have distinctive and pronounced flavours, and tend to be specialised in their use because of this. For example, rosemary goes well with lamb, fennel needs to be paired with fish, tarragon is the herb to use with eggs, and basil is especially good with tomatoes. Of course, they can be used with other foods as well, but

sparingly, because of their pungency.

The herbs mentioned so far are used in savoury dishes, but there are many others which can be used to flavour sweet recipes, and summer drinks including cordials, wines and punches. Angelica stems are easily prepared for candying, for cakes and trifles; caraway seeds are essential for the cake so popular with the Victorians; the leaves of sweet cicely can be added to fruit when cooking and will reduce, by at least half, the amount of sugar needed.

The cucumber-flavoured leaves of borage do wonders for wine punches, and its beautiful blue flowers, floating on the surface of white wine, are extremely decorative. The leaves of pineapple mint and lemon balm, and the orange-flavoured seeds of coriander, are some more delightful additions to cooling drinks.

Teas and tisanes made from herbs were formerly much used, and tisanes are still in Continental Europe, particularly in France and Germany. There is really no difference between them, except that teas tend to be drunk for refreshment, and tisanes for health reasons. Both are an infusion of leaves in boiling water.

Peppermint tea is still very popular, to help the digestion. Limeflower tea is sleep-inducing, and a tisane of cost-mary leaves is said to ease catarrh.

There are some less well-known herbs which really ought to be used by every cook; they are not difficult to grow, and plants or seeds are widely available.

The savories, winter and summer, are highly aromatic, so much so that they are almost a spice. They blend particularly well with all sorts of beans, and are used with broad beans in some Continental countries as much as mint sauce is used with lamb in Britain.

French sorrel leaves will pep up salads and make a tasty addition to all sorts of soups. They will make a deli-cious soup in their own right, mixed with stock, cream and a little onion.

The leaves of lovage added to soups and consommés provide the flavours of yeast and celery, and they can replace meat stock almost completely. The dried leaves and seeds mixed with vinegar, make a change from the con-ventional flavour of vinegar, and the liquor is a particularly good medium for pickling gerkins.

HOW TO MAKE BOUQUET GARNI

Using a bouquet garni is the classic way of flavouring casseroles, soups and sauces without leaving unwanted bits of plant in the dish.

Tie ingredients in muslin bag

Instructions
The traditional bouquet garni consists of a few sprigs of parsley, thyme and bay, tied in a muslin bag. Marjoram is frequently included and dill or tarragon would be suitable for many dishes.

Leave enough string to hang outside pot

Having chosen your herbs, cut one or two sprigs of each (remember that some herbs have very strong flavours) and place them on a square of muslin about 12.5cm (5in) square. Fold in the corners and tie the top of the 'bag' with a piece of string long enough to leave one end outside the pot. You can then remove the herbs comfortably.

Ornamental herbs

We tend to forget that herbs are not confined to culinary use and that they have medicinal and cosmetic use as well. It is amongst these that the most decorative kinds occur. Bergamot is a handsome herbaceous border plant, grown for its bright red, pink, mauve or white flowers. Lavender is another very ornamental herb; its fragrance has a slight edge on its beauty, but there are one or two lavender varieties almost without fragrance which are grown primarily for their flowers. Other ornamental plants, once mainly grown for their herbal properties, include southernwood, tansy, rue, marigold, borage, irises and honeysuckle. The bright yellow flowers of chamomile are still used for lightening hair.

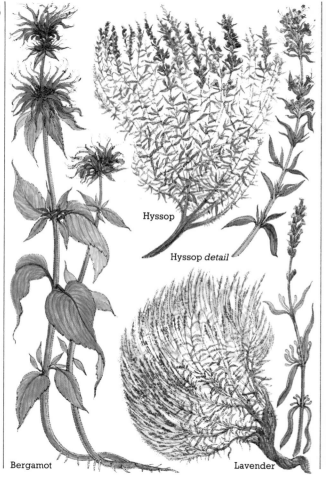

Hyssop

Hyssop *detail*

Bergamot

Lavender

Honeysuckle

Rue

Borage

Marigold

Lungwort

19

Herbs for decoration

If you are going to grow herbs at all, you will naturally want to make the most use of their ornamental qualities, and there are various ways in which you can exploit these to their greatest advantage. Which you choose depends on your reasons for growing herbs in the first place, and the size of your garden, as well as the usual garden limitations such as soil type, aspect and climate.

One of the most attractive arrangements is to collect your herbs together into one place and to design a herb garden along the lines of an old-fashioned one, so that you have a garden within a garden, with definite boundaries in the form of edgings to the beds, perhaps a hedge round the whole area, and paved or planted paths criss-crossing through it.

Another possibility is to give them their own long border, planting it like an herbaceous border, with the tall species at the back and a choice of herb that will give a succession of flowers or decorative leaves through the spring and summer. If you cannot spare the room for a whole border, they can well be mixed in to the herbaceous border. Many are grown as herbaceous perennials now – catmint, yellow gentian, iris to name just a few.

Don't forget that many herbs take very kindly to container-growing. Troughs, pots and tubs on a terrace or patio can all be filled with a herbal assortment. Lavender, sweet bay and rosemary look good in tubs, chives mixed with borage would produce an eye-catching effect when in flower, and marigolds mixed with nasturtiums and tansy would brighten up the dullest, most sunless day.

To get your herbs to look their most decorative, they need to have definition worked into their planting design, otherwise they will simply become a woolly green muddle. Give them precision by means of paved paths, box edgings, confine them within containers, and keep them well and unobtrusively staked. Cut them down low after flowering, and give them good soil so that they are strong, and do not flop about, and then your herbs will be a credit to you and a very attractive feature of the garden.

Herb flowers
colour check list

When considering the ornamental value of herbs in your garden, use the chart below to help in choosing flower colours. *See Planning, pages 26-27.*

HERB	FLOWER COLOUR	HERB	FLOWER COLOUR
Angelica	white	Iris (Orris)	white
Anise	yellow-white	Iris	violet-blue
Balm, lemon	white	Lavender	lavender
Basil	white	Lovage	yellowish green
Bay	yellow	Marigold	orange
Bergamot	red, pink	Marjoram	pink
Borage	blue	Mint	shades of purple
Burnet	green	Nasturtium	orange, yellow, red
Caraway	white	Parsley	green-yellow
Catmint	pale pink	Pennyroyal	reddish purple
Chamomile	white & yellow	Purslane	yellow
Chervil	white	Roses	pink
Chives	purple	Rosemary	pale blue
Comfrey	yellow or purple	Rue	yellow
Coriander	pale purple	Sage	pinkish white
Costmary	white	Savory	pale lilac
Dill	yellow	Skullcap	blue
Elder	white	Sorrel	pinkish green
Eyebright	white or lilac	Sweet Cicely	white
Fennel	yellow	Tansy .	yellow
Garlic	white	Tarragon	green-white
Gentian	yellow	Thyme	lilac
Honeysuckle	cream & rose pink	Valerian	pale pink
Hops	green	Vervain	pale lilac
Horseradish	white	Woad	yellow
Hyssop	pink, blue or white	Wormwood	green-yellow

The Physic garden

Herbs started life, so to speak, as medicinal plants grown during the Dark Ages and the Middle Ages by the monastic physicians, the medieval apothecaries, and the occasional layman or laywoman who had a leaning towards medicine and curing. There survives a plan of an ideal monastery and its gardens, made in about 980 AD, which shows the physic garden and names 15-20 plants to grow in it.

The process of discovering which plants improved one's health or alleviated an injury or illness must have been a long and painful one at the beginning, especially as some plants are exceedingly poisonous, for example hemlock and deadly nightshade. Nevertheless, as well as eating various parts of the plants to supply some of the daily food, primitive people also found out that they could cure themselves of some diseases by eating certain plants. As this information accumulated, specialists in the knowledge of healthgiving plants became part of the community.

For convenience's sake, such plants were cultivated in one place, and so the physic garden was as essential to the doctor as a chemist's shop is today.

The laboratory garden
The physic garden was
the place where the very
early herbalists and
apothecaries grew
medicinal plants for
making their 'patent'
cures. Many such gardens
belonged to monasteries.
A plan survives of the
monastery garden at St.
Gall, *above*. This
document is dated 820
AD. The physic garden in
the bottom half of the plan
contains lilies, roses and
fourteen beds of herbs.
The woodcut published in
Paris in 1500, *right,* shows
herbalists and
apothecaries in a very
scientific light. Their
researches are still taken
seriously: only recently it
has been discovered that
feverfew, *above left,* can
be used in curing migraine.

POTENTIAL POISONS

If you intend to use herbs for culinary, medicinal or cosmetic purposes, you must first make sure that the plants you intend to use are safe. Many plants, especially some of those with medicinal properties, are dangerous. Some can be fatal. Others are safe in mild doses but lethal in large quantities.

Foxglove
Digitalis purpurea, one of the most dangerous of garden plants. Its leaves contain a number of glucosides, including digitoxin and gitoxin which, although valuable in the treatment of heart disease, are very poisonous.

Henbane
Called *Hyoscyamus,* or hog's bean, by Dioscorides because pigs seemed to be the only creatures who could safely eat it. All parts of the plant are toxic, its main constituent being the alkaloid Hyoscyamine.

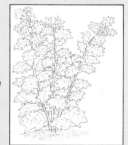

Common medicinal herbs

In the 20th century, herbs have not been used for medicinal purposes to anything like the same degree that they used to be, particularly from medieval times to the end of the 17th century. There was a revival of the use of some of them during the 1st and 2nd world wars, but since then synthetic drugs made in the laboratory have taken precedence. It has only been during the last few years that serious attention has been given to the possibility of using herbs on a greatly increased scale in the future.

However, some medicinal herbs have continued to be grown and their extracts used regularly, amongst them foxglove, *Digitalis officinalis;* it is a by-word for its usefulness in improving heart conditions. The opium or white poppy, *Papaver somniferum,* is still grown commercially to provide a sedative, and an analgesic. Tincture of opium was popularly known as Laudanum, and was much used by the Victorians.

Colchicum supplies colchicine, used in arthritic and rheumatic complaints; mistletoe has had good effects in the treatment of epilepsy. The essential ingredient of aspirin was originally extracted from willow, one of whose earliest botanic names was spiraea.

Plants which are easily grown by the gardener *(see the growing instructions)* and are said to be helpful for a number of minor complaints include comfrey, eyebright, yellow gentian, hops, marigold, parsley, purslane, sage and valerian. Parsley water helps freckles, hop pillows overcome insomnia, sage tea can be tried for alleviating sore throats, and a comfrey leaf poultice is thought to relieve boils and sprains.

Do remember that if you would like to try any kind of herbal mixture as a remedy for ill-health, of whatever sort, you must be exceedingly careful. Many medicinal herbs are potentially poisonous; what may well be a mild purgative in small quantities, could be a killer in large quantities.

Some other common plants which supply medicinal ingredients are the castor-oil plant *(Ricinus communis)*, autumn crocus *(Colchicum autumnale)*, mistletoe and willow. Castor-oil seems to have been used as a purgative since the days of ancient Egypt, but was also thought by the Greeks of Pliny's day to have other powers, such as a tonic for hair, and curing diseases of the joints.

SOME MEDICINAL HERBS AND THEIR USES

Autumn Crocus *Colchicum autumnale*	Toxic – used in curing gout and arthritis
Belladonna *Atropa belladona*	Narcotic – used in sedatives
Bittersweet *Solanum dulcamara*	Toxic – used for curing skin diseases
Mistletoe *Viscum album*	Used in treating high blood pressure
Opium poppy *Papaver somniferum*	Narcotic – used in sedatives/pain killers
Valerian *Valeriana officinalis*	Used in the treatment of nervous diseases

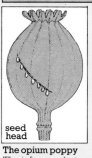

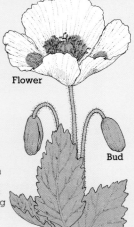

seed head

Flower

Bud

The opium poppy
The infamous, but medicinally valuable, drug is extracted from the wall of the dried seed head. The seeds do not contain anything other than a harmless oil.

Herb garden design

Herb gardens are, by tradition, formally designed. If you come across any of the plans used in medieval herb gardens, you will find that the beds are geometrical, and surrounded by clipped edgings or outlined with a border of stone or pebbles. The Elizabethan 'knot' garden is still most attractive, consisting of variously shaped small beds, laid out in a complicated design, and edged with trimmed box. Curved beds filling a circle, angular beds in a square pattern, or beds forming the spokes of a wheel, also provide the necessary definition. A sun-dial, bird bath, pool, bee-hive or garden seat are suitable focal points and a small lawn can add to the atmosphere of peace and tranquillity.

Informal gardens
Herb gardens do not have to be rigidly laid out in symmetrical patterns to be attractive. The very casual arrangement, *top*, looks well in a small garden, while the clustering foliage of sage, mint and hyssop, *above*, needs only the stone pedestal to give it form and depth.

PLANNING YOUR HERB GARDEN

Plan your herb garden on squared paper first, measured to scale. Blend the colours of the flowers and leaves *see chart page 21*. Remember that the plants will grow horizontally as well as vertically, and will need spacing accordingly.

Focal points
The herb garden at Cranborne Manor, Dorset, *left*, is exceptionally large and benefits considerably from the positioning of the ornamental urn. The rose standards encircling the urn and the foreshortening effect of the yew hedge help to give the garden structure. This is only one of many famous herb gardens in Europe, where the practice of creating modern herb gardens is increasing in popularity.

Planning – basic considerations

Once you have decided on the shape and appearance of the herb garden, there are some practical details which it is advisable to consider before actually getting down to the business of digging and planting.

The site: herbs more than most plants, need well-drained soil. It need not be particularly fertile, in fact many aromatic herbs are the better for being grown slightly starved, but they cannot abide wet feet. Even parsley and mint, which like moisture, do not relish waterlogging.

Plant herbs which have the same needs together. For instance rosemary and lavender naturally grow in rocky soil and blazing sun; horseradish needs heavy, moist soil and angelica prefers shade and closeness to running water.

Also group herbs according to their final heights. Some such as lovage and fennel, grow very tall, up to 150cm (5ft) and more; if you put these in front of eyebright or marigolds, the smaller plants will be swamped, as well as invisible.

Put the low-growing herbs, chives, tansy or hyssop, etc., at the front of the beds as edgings, if you do not intend to have a formal hedge.

Annual herbs are conveniently grown in patches, not dotted about in groups of two or three plants. They look better, and grow better, and you can put the perennial kinds in between, or grow the perennials in beds of their own.

Your paths can be surfaced in various ways. Inert materials – paving, bricks, grit, shingle, sand, pebbles – will need little upkeep beyond weed control and occasional levelling. It is as well to calculate how much of any of these you will need beforehand; bricks and paving can be laid down in a great variety of designs, and cost will vary according to material and area. Remember that paths are an important part of herb gardens, not only for appearances, but also for regular access.

If grass paths are required, they will need regular cutting and attention just as a lawn does; herbal paths, however, need only to be trimmed every few weeks, but will not take a great deal of traffic. They will probably need patching every season and renewing every three or four years.

PLANTING SCHEMES

The chart below selects, from the herbs dealt with in this book, those which are most useful in, and suitable for, an average garden. This may help in planning and designing your garden.

CULINARY	MEDICINAL	ORNAMENTAL
Basil	Chamomile	Bergamot
Bay	Comfrey	Borage
Chervil	Elder	Catmint
Chives	Eyebright	Honeysuckle
Garlic	Gentian	Iris
Marjoram	Hyssop	Lavender
Mint	Rue	Marigold
Parsley	Skullcap	Nasturtium
Rosemary	Tansy	Roses
Sage	Valerian	Rosemary
Tarragon	Vervain	Sage
Thyme	Wormwood	Tansy

Wild herbs

There are many plants which we overlook and dismiss as weeds now, which were once used for a variety of herbal purposes. For instance, the insignificant little *Euphrasia officinalis,* or eyebright, is a common weed beside paths and fields in summer, and yet it was once, and still is, commended for eye troubles. Tansy grows wild in hedges and thickets; chamomile is common on sandy soil, honeysuckle festoons hedges and trees, and elder is forever being rooted out by exasperated gardeners.

Lesser celandine is considered to be a great pest if it grows in gardens, yet its other common name of Pilewort indicates its old medical value. Dock leaves are still rubbed on to nettle stings by country children, dandelions were used for liver complaints, even daisies were used in healing wounds.

Nettles were eaten like spinach or used to relieve coughs, ground ivy was supposed to help with nervous headaches and broom was actually used for making brooms. Its flowers formed part of an ointment to cure gout. Dyers Greenweed was used for supplying a deep yellow dye and, mixed with woad, formed a brilliant green.

29

Herbs of the hedgerows

Whenever you take a country walk, remember that practically all the plants you see growing wild in fields, woods and paths were once what we now call herbs, and had some specific and practical use in everyday life. It is worth taking a good herbal with you for identification. You will find that almost any plant you see has its own history, extending back as far as the Dark Ages and beyond, and supplies one ingredient or another for human needs.

Wild herbs and their uses
1 **Nettle** – coughs, skin troubles
2 **Sweetbriar rose** – vitamins A/C
3 **Dandelion** – liver complaints
4 **Celandine** – haemorrhoids
5 **Eyebright** – eye troubles
6 **Woad** – healing wounds
7 **Dock** – soothing stings
8 **Chamomile** – toothache
9 **Feverfew** – migraine
10 **Ox-eye daisy** – healing wounds

31

Herbs for containers

Herbs lend themselves very well to container cultivation and, indeed, it is really the only way to grow the mints if you do not want the garden overrun with peppermint, garden mint, ginger mint and so on. Most of them are smallish plants, without a large root system, and so fit comfortably into pots, tubs, troughs, bowls, grow-bags, hanging baskets, old stone sinks – in fact anything which can be provided with drainage holes and is portable.

The kitchen herbs are particularly convenient grown like this, because you can set them just outside the house ready to hand the instant the recipe demands it, or you can bring them in to the kitchen window-sill for the winter.

Of course all the other kinds can be grown like this – cosmetic, medicinal and aromatic – but of these, probably the aromatic and fragrant ones will be the only species you will want to bring indoors. Mobile herbs have advantages over the others, in that you can chase the sun, tailor the soil to their needs, keep them away from cold, and use them to cover up some dull, unplantable patches of the garden. Most important of all, however, is having *fresh* herbs available throughout the year.

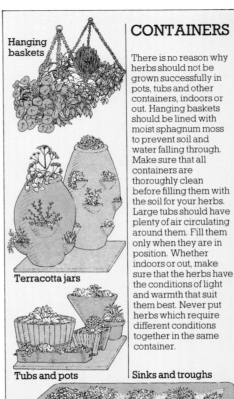

Hanging baskets

Terracotta jars

Tubs and pots

Sinks and troughs

CONTAINERS

There is no reason why herbs should not be grown successfully in pots, tubs and other containers, indoors or out. Hanging baskets should be lined with moist sphagnum moss to prevent soil and water falling through. Make sure that all containers are thoroughly clean before filling them with the soil for your herbs. Large tubs should have plenty of air circulating around them. Fill them only when they are in position. Whether indoors or out, make sure that the herbs have the conditions of light and warmth that suit them best. Never put herbs which require different conditions together in the same container.

How to grow herbs in containers

Growing in pots

In general, the average herbaceous kind of herb will grow best grouped in a trough, window-box or grow-bag. Some will do well grown singly in individual pots. However, the smallest pot-size for good results is 10cm (4in) diameter, even for parsley, which many people cram into a 7cm (3in) pot and then wonder why it grows badly.

Soil/compost

You will not go far wrong if you use the John Innes composts or an equivalent proprietary compost. The soilless composts are particularly good for encouraging root development, though plants will need to be liquid-fed. To make up your own, use a mixture of 7 parts loam, 3 parts peat and 2 parts course sand; and add to 36 litres (1 bushel) of this, 120g (4oz) of a balanced fertilizer containing nitrogen, phosphorus and potassium, and 21 g (¾ oz) of chalk.

Position/potting/watering

Put your containers in the sun or shade, according to the needs of the plants, and avoid draughty passages and windswept corners. Shelter and/or sun will be much kinder to the plants.

When you pot your plants, make sure they are in the centre, leave a space at the top of the container for watering at least 1.2cm (½in) deep, and firm the compost down well. Water them in and allow the surplus water to drain through, then put the container in a shady place until they begin to lengthen their shoots.

When you water again, wait until the compost surface shows dry, and then fill up the space at the top of the pot, allowing drainage as before.

Growing indoors

Like any other plant grown in the home, you should suit the plant to the conditions. In order to flourish, herbs in the house should be close to a window so that they get the best possible light.

Those that are hardy should be put in a cool room for the winter; the slightly tender kinds will do better with a little warmth, 10-13°C (50-55°F). Tarragon is an exception; keep it cool so that it remains dormant, otherwise it outgrows its strength and dies.

Some good culinary herbs to grow indoors are: parsley, chives, pot marjoram, basil, mint, sage and thyme.

Types of herb

Perennials

Quite a lot of herbs die down in autumn though they will sprout again the following year. These are herbaceous perennials; they will live for several years. Some perennial plants are woody, losing their leaves in autumn. Others are evergreen, and leaves can be gathered all year round. Perennials, whether herbaceous or woody, are usually grown from small plants formed from stem cuttings, division of plants or layering.

Annuals

There are also herbs which not only die down in autumn, but in fact die completely. These are called annuals, grown from seed sown in late summer or spring. They flower and seed within twelve months of seed being sown, and then die. If leaves of these are wanted for winter use, they have to be dried.

Biennials

Biennials flower early in the second summer after sowing and then die. However, they are hardy enough to live through the first winter, so fresh leaves can often be taken from them; parsley is one example.

THE PARTS TO USE

The parts of herbal plants which are commonly used are the leaves. The seeds of some are used to flavour food and drink, and the roots of a few are ground up or extracted to provide the essential ingredient.

HERB	PARTS USED	HERB	PARTS USED
Anise	seeds	Iris (Orris)	roots
Angelica	all	Iris	roots
Balm	leaves	Lavender	leaves/flowers
Basil	leaves	Lovage	leaves
Bay	leaves	Marigold	flowers
Bergamot	leaves/flowers	Marjoram	leaves
Borage	leaves/flowers	Mint	leaves
Burnet	leaves	Nasturtium	leaves/seeds
Caraway	seeds	Parsley	leaves
Catmint	leaves	Pennyroyal	leaves
Chamomile	flowers	Purslane	leaves
Chervil	leaves	Roses	hips/petals
Chives	leaves	Rosemary	leaves
Comfrey	leaves/roots	Rue	leaves
Coriander	seeds	Sage	leaves
Costmary	leaves	Savory	leaves
Dill	leaves/seeds	Skullcap	roots
Elder	flowers/fruit	Sorrel	leaves
Eyebright	all	Sweet Cicely	leaves
Fennel	leaves	Tansy	leaves/flowers
Garlic	bulb	Tarragon	leaves
Gentian	roots	Thyme	leaves
Honeysuckle	leaves	Valerian	roots
Hops	flowers	Vervain	leaves
Horseradish	roots	Woad	leaves
Hyssop	leaves	Wormwood	leaves

Buying seeds and plants

If the herbs you are to grow are annuals or biennials, it is usually least expensive and most satisfactory to grow the plants from seed. You may be able to find some biennials as small plants at the local nursery and also, in late spring, some tender annuals.

Seed can be obtained from garden shops, the gardening departments of chain stores and ironmongers, and the garden centres, or you can obtain it mail-order from seedsmen. Their catalogues will often have a special section for herbs, together with prices, and you can order them well in advance.

The perennials, on the other hand, although many can be grown from seed, are better started from small plants bought in spring or autumn. It may be a year, when grown from seed, before they can be used, but small plants can be lightly harvested within two months. By all means try it, if speed is not important.

Look for plants which have strong stems, leaves a good deep green, and roots which fill the container comfortably. The roots should not be wound round and round the outside of the soil-ball or protrude from the drainage holes to any great degree.

ADVICE ON BUYING

Buying seeds
The increasing popularity of herbs means that it is now possible to buy seeds for herbs from the leading seed merchants. Some will present difficulties, in which case the best policy will be to try a herb farm – or settle for a plant.

Storing seeds
Any glass jar with a tight fitting lid will be satisfactory for storing seed. Make sure that it is clean and dry (preferably sterilised), and clearly labelled. Using seeds collected from your own plants is often quite successful with herbs.

Buying plants
Herb plants are easily obtainable from garden centres and specialist herb farms. It should even be possible to buy some of the more unusual examples – although it may necessitate a lengthy search. Do not buy plants which have outgrown their containers.

Soil preparation & general cultivation

One of the greatest assets that herbs have, as far as the gardener is concerned, is that they are easy to grow. Many are hardy plants, native to temperate climates, and with these it may be a matter of keeping them in check, rather than fighting to get them to grow.

Soil type is not crucial. Ideally, it should be light, the kind that allows rain to drain through it rather than collect in puddles, and it need not be rich, just an ordinary loam. The heavier soils will grow herbs, but the addition of grit or coarse sand, dug in before planting at about 3½kg per sq m (7lb per sq yd) will result in less leafy and more flowery plants, as the moisture is en-

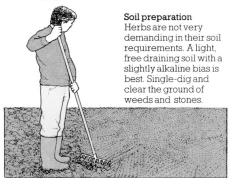

Soil preparation
Herbs are not very demanding in their soil requirements. A light, free draining soil with a slightly alkaline bias is best. Single-dig and clear the ground of weeds and stones.

couraged to pass down into the sub soil.

Worked-out soil in old gardens in towns, or very poor stony soils will be the better for the digging-in of rotted manure or garden compost in late winter, and a dressing of a slow-acting organic fertilizer such as hoof and horn or bonemeal at 60-90g per sq m (2-3 oz per sq yd).

Plants can be grown from seed sown in mid spring, outdoors if hardy, under cover in gentle heat if tender.

For outdoor seed-sowing, make sure the soil has been evenly dug and levelled, clear it of weeds and large stones and rake the surface so that it breaks down into the consistency of breadcrumbs. Sow the seeds thinly in rows or patches, cover with 6mm (¾in) of soil and water-in with a fine spray. Protect from birds.

If starting with plants, use a hand fork or trowel to dig a hole large enough to take the roots spread out naturally, crumble the soil back over them, and firm-in well, then water.

As the plants grow, thin the seedlings, and tie those plants which need it to unobtrusive supports. This is important as herbs very quickly look a mess if not stiffened in some way. On very stony or sandy soils, put a thin covering or mulch of rotted garden compost round the plants when the soil is moist, in late spring or early summer.

Unless seed is wanted, flower stems should be cut off. Most herbal seeds are ripe round late July or August, and many are best sown then, to produce the next season's plants, as their ability to germinate drops quickly after autumn.

Troubles are very few. Greenfly may be a pest in crowded conditions, especially on parsley and chives. Mint sometimes gets infested with rust fungus disease, and should then be burnt and replaced with fresh plants in a different place. Bay trees are popular with scale insects on the bark and undersides of leaves; scrape the small brown scales off with a finger nail.

Sometime in autumn cut down the dead stems, and clear off the old leaves, if you like tidiness, or leave them on the plant for protection against cold until spring. Clear weeds and hoe the soil lightly. Put cloches over those whose season you want to prolong, or those which must have a barrier against frost.

PLANTING OUT

The best times for planting out herbs which have been raised in containers are spring and autumn. But you can do it at any time of year if the weather is not too cold or too dry. Soak the plants on the day before planting and make sure that the soil which is going to receive them is moist. Gently knock the base of the container to remove the plant and soil ball. Carefully loosen the outside roots but do not break up the soil ball. Make sure that the planting hole is big enough to accommodate the soil ball with its surface just below ground level. Fill in with soil, firm down well and water in.

Gently knock plant free

Loosen root ball

Fill in, firm soil, water in

Plant below ground level

Harvesting

The herbs which are grown for leaves will usually provide fresh foliage between mid spring and mid autumn; some of them, such as chives, parsley, bay and sage, will provide it for most of the year.

If they have been grown from seed, it is better to wait until the young plants are growing well before you start to denude them, and then for a few weeks take only the outer, oldest leaves. Perennials can be harvested soon after growth starts again in spring, but should be left alone after the end of early autumn.

If you want to harvest your herbs for drying and storing there are optimum times in the plant's life when this can be done. Leaves should be gathered just before the flower buds start to open. Flowers should be picked when they have fully opened, but just before they are completely mature, and certainly before they begin to fade or discolour.

Seedheads are cut when the seeds are ripe, i.e. when they are beginning to shake loose. Many are brown when ripe, some are yellowish or black. Fruits should just have reached their full colour, and roots are dug up at the end of the growing season.

Drying and storing

Herbs should be gathered early on a dry, calm morning, after the dew has gone. Take great care not to bruise them in any way, and lay them in a flat-bottomed basket. Use a really sharp knife to avoid bruising, and transfer them quickly to the drying area.

All this care in cutting and handling is aimed at conserving as much as possible of the essential oils in the material. Once the plants have been injured the oils, being volatile, begin to escape, and the herbal qualities fall rapidly. You should deal with the plants quickly but gently, for the best results. Cover them to keep out the light, and take into the drying place. This can be an airing cupboard, the plate-warming compartment of a stove, part of a greenhouse suitably darkened, a cooling oven, or a clothes-drying cabinet.

Leaves and flowers will retain their aroma and colour (green or otherwise) best if dried as quickly, but carefully, as possible. Hence a temperature of 21-32°C (70-90°F), combined with ventilation to prevent humidity, will produce the best results. Start them at about 32°C (90°F) for 24 hours and then allow it to fall; it should never rise above 39°C (100°F). Lay the material in single layers on trays, or in shallow boxes or wooden frames with nylon or cotton netting or muslin stretched across. Do not allow any light to reach the herbs while drying, and turn them daily.

The time each herb takes to dry varies – it may be 2-7 days or longer. Leaves and flowers are, however, finished when they are brittle and flaky. If powdery, they are too dry, if still flexible, they are not ready. The stems will crack, not bend, when they are ready. Roots should be similarly dry right through, in no way soft or spongy in the centre. Seeds should be dry when collected and can be cleaned and stored at once.

Storing

Once drying is finished, let the material cool, strip away unwanted stalks, and crumble or chop the leaves into small pieces. Put at once into air-tight, light-proof containers.

Wooden jars, with screw tops, boxes lined with aluminium foil, or opaque glass bottles with tightly fitting lids, are all good. Label them and date them, and put one herb in each container, unless you wish to have a particular mixture for cooking or making tisanes.

HARVESTING/DRYING/STORING

Drying large leaves

Drying small leaves

Selecting large leaves

Crumbling small leaves

When to harvest
Leaves should be picked just before the flowers open – and on a warm, dry morning, after the dew has gone.

Drying
Large leaf plants should be spread on racks or trays and covered with a sheet of muslin. Select the best leaves and put them in a warm, dark, airy place. Turn the herbs daily. Small leaf plants can be put, whole, into paper bags or newspaper and hung to dry. When they are dry, the leaves can be crumbled for storing in jars.

Storing herbs
Herbs should be stored in light-proof containers in order to preserve colour and natural oils. Lids must be tight fitting.

Making potpourris

Potpourri is a delightful reminder of summer's colour and fragrance. The petals of any perfumed flowers and the aromatic or fragrant leaves of plants such as the pelargoniums (geraniums), rosemary, costmary or woodruff can all be used.

Roses, violets, lavender, jasmine, carnations and orange blossom are some of the best flowers; the most fragrant roses are usually the deep crimson ones or the damask roses *(Rosa damascena)*. For extra and lasting colour you can put in some of the non-fragrant flowers such as delphiniums or marigolds.

Whatever is used, the leaves and flowers should be gathered and dried as previously described. Inadequate drying results in the appearance of mould and an unpleasant smell.

The petals and leaves are put in layers into a jar, with a mixture of bay salt or ordinary salt and mixed spices sprinkled on to each 1.2cm (½in) thick layer. Bay salt can still be bought from the older-established chemists.

The spices can be any sort of mixture, according to the recipe, and consist of such ingredients as powdered cinnamon, allspice, orris-root, cloves, orange peel and so on, already mixed with oil of lavender, bergamot, lemon, geranium, etc.

Put the potpourri to mature in an air- and light-tight container for about a month, and stir it every few days. Then transfer it to bowls or glass jars, when it will perfume a room for many months.

Remember, that if you use a predominance of one flower, the potpourri will be redolent of that, and that roses are the basis for all mixtures. Incidentally, it is possible to buy a ready-made up mixture of spices, oils and fixatives, to add to the petals and leaves.

There are many traditional recipes for potpourri, and the variations of ingredients can be considerable, but one of the old mixtures is as follows: "Dry the flowers of damask and cabbage roses *(R. centifolia)*, lavender, carnation, woodruff, rosemary and violet, and the leaves of bay, sweet briar roses, lemon balm, thyme and mint. Add strips of lemon and orange peel. Mix 1lb salt, ½lb bay salt, ½oz storax, 6 drams orris-root, a grated nutmeg, ½ teaspoon powdered cloves, ½ teaspoon allspice and 1oz oil bergamot, adding the oil after the other ingredients have been thoroughly mixed."

HOW TO MAKE A POTPOURRI

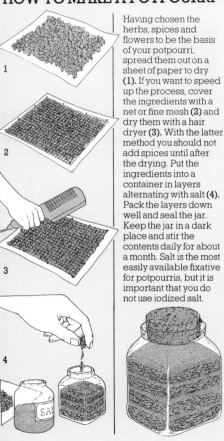

Having chosen the herbs, spices and flowers to be the basis of your potpourri, spread them out on a sheet of paper to dry (1). If you want to speed up the process, cover the ingredients with a net or fine mesh (2) and dry them with a hair dryer (3). With the latter method you should not add spices until after the drying. Put the ingredients into a container in layers alternating with salt (4). Pack the layers down well and seal the jar. Keep the jar in a dark place and stir the contents daily for about a month. Salt is the most easily available fixative for potpourris, but it is important that you do not use iodized salt.

Herbs for cosmetics

In line with the herb revival in cooking and medicine has come one in cosmetics. Natural ways of improving, healing and beautifying the skin and hair are becoming more and more popular. Certainly, there is nothing against using chamomile flowers to lighten hair, rosemary leaf infusions on oily hair, lemon balm water as a skin tonic, and soapwort (Saponaria officinalis) to take the place of soap.

A great number of plants were used to supply cosmetics in earlier times. They were easily come by and easily made up by infusing with water, or pounding and mixing with oils.

Herbal cosmetics are particularly useful for people with allergies who may react badly to the artificial additives used in modern cosmetics. Many of them have a therapeutic effect on the skin, healing spots and encouraging cell growth, as well as being antiseptic and supplying minerals and vitamins.

Rouge can be made from gromwell, and the flowers of saffron and marigold mixed together and infused will produce a red dye. Freckles can be bleached out with chickweed or horseradish, and cucumbers provide an excellent astringent.

Infusions and oils

Basically, making an infusion of a herb is very simple; it merely consists of pouring freshly boiled water on to the leaves, fresh or dried, and leaving the mixture to stand or infuse for about five minutes, to draw out the flavour and the essence of the herb. A tea made in this way is drunk mainly for its refreshing and restoring qualities; a tisane is made of herbs which actively help to encourage sleep, overcome digestive orders, and calm the nerves. Tisanes are much more therapeutic but nonetheless pleasant to drink, especially those made of lime, peppermint or chamomile.

Herbal oils are just as easily made. Corn or olive oil mixed with wine vinegar is the basis for the mixture. Pour the oil and vinegar over the herb leaves in a glass bottle, stopper, and shake hard once a day, for two weeks. Put the bottle in the sun or a warm place. Then strain through muslin, replace the old herbs with fresh ones, and continue until the oil smells strongly of the herb. It is easy to make lavender oil in this way, also rosemary or sage, and any strongly aromatic leaf can be used. The resultant oil can be used for culinary or cosmetic purposes.

HOW TO MAKE AN INFUSION

You can use dried or fresh herbs to make teas and infusions. If you are using dried herbs, one 5ml spoon (1 teaspoon) per cup, will be enough. If you are using fresh herbs, three 5ml spoons, (3 teaspoons) per cup will be needed. Fresh herbs should be crushed before adding boiling water. As in any form of tea making, the water should be at boiling point when it is poured onto the leaves. The infusion should be covered and left to stand for about five minutes before drinking. Herbs do not contain stimulants, such as tannin, so they tend to be more soothing and relaxing than tea.

HERBS FOR TEAS

Balm	Lime flower
Bergamot	Lovage
Borage	Marigold
Burnet	Parsley
Chamomile	Pennyroyal
Costmary	Peppermint
Elder	Rose hips
Hops	Savory
Hyssop	Valerian

The following pages contain simple growing instructions for fifty herbs which are suitable for garden cultivation

Anise

(Culinary) *Pimpinella anisum*

Description	slightly tender annual; flowers midsummer; height 45cm (18in)
Uses	seeds are used for flavouring cakes and bread, creams and sweets, also to marinate fish and to flavour liqueurs and cordials; the herb is widely grown commercially in Mediterranean areas
Site/soil	sunny and sheltered, light but rich soil
Sow/plant	sow outdoors in mid spring, thin to 30cm (1ft) apart; sow in containers in warmth and plant out in late spring if the season is cold
Cultivate	keep free from weeds and protect young plants against frost and cold wind; roots can be divided in spring
Harvest	seeds, when ripe and greyish brown, in autumn; needs warmth, and usually only ripens in warm summers, hence the need for a really sheltered and sunny place
History	a very old herb, cultivated by the ancient Egyptians, then by the Greeks and Romans, and in Britain from the 14th century. It is said to avert the 'Evil Eye' and was considered by Gerard to help 'the yeoxing or hicket (hiccough)', he also believed, more generally, that it was 'good against belchings and upraidings of the stomacke'; aniseed flavoured bread, common today, was baked in Greece over 2,000 years ago

Anise *plant*

A digestive tonic
The seeds of anise (aniseed) are very effective in easing digestive complaints. Make an infusion by pouring a cup of boiling water onto 2.5ml (½ teaspoon) of the seeds and let it stand for five minutes. It makes a good bedtime drink.

Seed pod

Angelica

(Culinary) *Angelica archangelica*

Angelica

Description	ornamental, short-lived, hardy perennial which dies down in autumn; flowers in late spring–early summer; height 150-180cm (5-6ft)
Uses	young stems candied and used for cake decorating; tips and young leaves cooked with rhubarb and gooseberries offset their acidity – the proportions are about 60g (2oz) to ½kg (1lb) fruit; the seeds are used commercially for flavouring Vermouth and Chartreuse; all parts of the plant can be used, including the roots, which have a delicate flavour when cooked with butter
Site/soil	moist soil and a slightly shaded place, sheltered from wind
Sow/plant	sow seed late summer, thin to 15cm (6in), then to 60cm (2ft) in the 2nd year, finally to 150cm (5ft); buy plants in autumn and spring
Cultivate	keep well watered in dry weather and remove main stems before they flower unless seeds are wanted; the plant will die after flowering and setting seed; stake in windy situations
History	obtains its name because it is said to bloom on May 8 in the older calendar, the day of St Michael the Archangel, and hence an antidote to witchcraft and spells; once called the 'root of the Holy Ghost', and much used medicinally; it was thought to be an effective cure for respiratory complaints and the root was widely used to ward off plague; angelica is one of the most widespread herbs

Candied Angelica
Use first year stems – cutting them into 12cm (5 in) lengths and boiling them in syrup. Leave for 24 hours, then boil again until the stems turn a bright green. Use them as sweets or cake decorations.

Angelica *root*

45

Balm, lemon

(Culinary and medicinal) *Melissa officinalis*

Description	hardy herbaceous perennial, dying down in autumn; flowers midsummer–early autumn; height 45-60cm (1½-2ft)
Uses	lemon-flavoured leaves can be added to custards, rice and other milk puddings, wine cups, crabapple jelly, melon, fruit salads. Balm or melissa tea made from dried leaves is said to be calming and relaxing, and helpful in fending off incipient headaches; dried leaves can be used in potpourri
Site/soil	any, within reason
Sow/plant	sow seeds outdoors in spring and thin in stages to 60cm (2ft); plant root divisions with buds or shoots on each in autumn or spring
Cultivate	very easily grown, merely keep free from weeds when young; seeds freely, remove flowers to encourage leaf development
Harvest	strip leaves as required, but not from young plants until midsummer; can be cut down to about 30cm (1ft) in early summer, late summer and end of early autumn, on a cool dull day just before flowering, when the leaves will contain the maximum amount of essential oil
History	known also as the 'bee herb' it was thought by Pliny that bees: 'when they are strayed away, they do find their way home by it.' It was always held in great esteem from ancient times for all sorts of nervous complaints, and for helping to heal wounds and injuries because of its antiseptic qualities

Lemon balm

Balm cordial
13g (½oz) of balm leaves, together with leaves of other aromatic and culinary herbs, such as mint, hyssop, basil and sage, should be steeped in alcohol for 10 days. Strain, and put into bottles with tightly fitting stoppers. This makes a drink which is very soothing to the digestive system.

Lemon balm *leaf detail*

Basil

(Culinary) *Ocimum basilicum*

Basil

Description	tender annual; flowers late summer; height 30cm (1ft)
Uses	distinctively and pungently flavoured leaves are splendid with tomatoes or any dish containing tomatoes; used also in omelettes, cheese and fish dishes, but can be used sparingly to give many recipes a little extra quality of flavour; also used in curries in India
Site/soil	warm, sunny, sheltered, with well-drained soil
Sow	sow seed in warmth, 16-18°C (60-65°F) in mid spring, sow 2 or 3 to a 5cm (2in) peat pot or block, remove all but the largest and plant pot complete after hardening off in early summer, 20cm (8in) apart
Cultivate	keep well watered, and in dry hot summers water daily, but allow soil to dry out between waterings; pinch out tips to prevent flowering
Harvest	strip leaves as required; remove for drying just before flowering, then cut down as quickly as possible
History	seems to have been loved or hated in almost equal quantities, some swearing by its medicinal and culinary qualities, others saying that it damaged the eyesight and dulled the wits. The name *basilicum* was muddled with *basiliscus,* a basilisk, a fabulous reptile hatched by a serpent from a cock's egg; from this it was said to cure serpent's bites. In some Mediterranean countries basil is a symbol of evil, but in the East it is greatly respected.

Basil in pots
Bush basil *(Ocimum minimum)* which is both smaller and hardier than the sweet basil, makes a good pot plant for the kitchen. Its uses are much the same as those of sweet basil.

Pinching out tip

Bay, sweet

(Culinary) (*Laurus nobilis*)

Description	ornamental, slightly tender, evergreen tree, flowers late spring, followed by black berries; height 3m (10ft), spread 6-9m (20-30ft).
Uses	strongly aromatic leaves are dried and used as part of bouquet garni, or alone for flavouring meat casseroles, particularly beef, or fish; also in many other savoury dishes; half or one leaf at a time is ample
Site/soil	sunny, sheltered, most reasonable soils; mature trees in such situations will survive hard winters
Sow/plant	plant one or two-year old plants in mid–late spring; one is sufficient
Cultivate	no special cultivation required; grows well in tubs, provided they are well protected against frost, because the roots are sensitive to cold in such conditions. Formal specimens can be clipped to various shapes, e.g. ball, pyramid; do this in late summer; propagation is difficult, but it can be achieved by layering in mid-summer
Harvest	leaves at any time in the year, but early in the day for drying; can be dried in an oven which is cooling after being used
History	the leaves provided the wreaths for heroes and poets, hence the term 'poet laureate'. Bay was thought to give protection against lightning, and Culpeper said that 'it resisteth witchcraft very potently'; the leaves were once thought to be a cure for almost any illness

Sweet bay *detail*

A tree of many uses
John Parkinson, writing in 1629, said: 'The Bay leaves are of a necessary use as any other in the garden or orchard... both for honest civil uses and for physic, yea, both for the sick and the sound, both for the living and the dead... so that from the cradle to the grave we still have use of it, we still have need of it.'

Bergamot

(Mainly medicinal) *Monarda didyma*

Description	ornamental, hardy herbaceous perennial; flowers early summer–early autumn; there are red, pink and purple-flowered kinds; height 60-90cm (2-3ft)
Uses	aromatic leaves used fresh or dried to make Oswego tea; infuse 3 teaspoons of chopped fresh, or 1 teaspoon of dried, per cup, with boiling water; induces deep and relaxing sleep; dried red flowers can also be used for tea. Can be used in summer drinks and shredded in salads, also in pot pourri
Site/soil	a little shade, and moist soil
Sow/plant	plant in spring or autumn, sow seed in spring and thin, transplant in autumn; space 60cm (2ft) apart for final positions
Cultivate	keep well watered in dry weather; dig up and divide in autumn every year, using the outside pieces; cuttings can be taken and rooted any time in late summer
Harvest	strip leaves as required from early summer onwards, also the flowers, and dry them slowly, so that the colour is kept
History	a North American plant, it was used by the Oswego Indians to make tea, and was the tea drunk by patriotic Americans at the time of the Boston Tea Party; sometimes called Bee Balm, because the flowers secrete a good deal of nectar; the flavour of the leaves is reminiscent of the Bergamot orange, from Bergamo in Italy

Bergamot *plant*

Other uses of bergamot
Bergamot is one of the most useful plants to have in your herbaceous border. Quite apart from the attraction of its striking red and pink flowers, and its capacity to draw bees to the garden, it has several indoor uses. The flowers are good for cutting, it makes a very relaxing tea, and it is an excellent herb for potpourris.

Bergamot *leaf detail*

Borage

(Culinary) *Borago officinalis*

Borage *plant*

Description	ornamental, hardy annual; flowers early summer–early autumn; height 30-60cm (1-2ft)
Uses	fresh leaves taste of cucumber and can be added, with the flowers, to summer drinks, salads and fruit salads, cooked cabbage, and pea soup; flowers can be candied, or dried for pot pourri
Site/soil	sun or a little shade; no special soil requirements
Sow/plant	sow seed any time from spring to autumn and thin to about 30cm (1ft) apart
Cultivate	very easily grown and no special cultivation required; once introduced to the garden, borage will self-sow and there will always be some plants present
Harvest	strip leaves as required from about 8 weeks after germination; in mild seasons and districts borage may still be growing and flowering in late autumn; drying is difficult to do at home, but the leaves are best used fresh
History	borage was thought to be the herb of courage in ancient Greece and was floated in stirrup cups offered to departing Crusaders; Gerard quotes an old Latin rhyme which translates to: 'I, Borage, bring alwaies courage.' Culpeper recommended it for the treatment of 'putrid and pestilential fever, and the venom of serpents'. The old country name of Bee Bread points to its attraction for bees, part of which is the beautiful blue flowers

Medicinal values
Borage is one of those plants which has been reputed, in many countries, to cure practically everything. Even today it is recommended by herbalists for the treatment of influenza, rheumatism, skin diseases and respiratory complaints. Whether this is true or not (and if it is, the stem of the plant becomes more important than the leaves), there is no doubt that the herb is an effective diuretic. But this should not deter you from adding a few leaves and flowers to summer drinks.

Burnet, salad

(Culinary) *Sanguisorba minor*

Description	low growing hardy herbaceous perennial, nearly evergreen; inconspicuous flowers early summer–early autumn; height (flower stems), 60-90cm (2-3ft)
Uses	fresh leaves are cucumber-flavoured and are very pleasant to add to summer drinks, green or fruit salads, mushroom and bean soups
Site/soil	sun or shade, soil preferably chalky
Sow/plant	sow seed outdoors in mid spring no deeper than 1.2cm (½in), and thin to about 23-30cm (9-12in) apart, or sow when ripe in late summer–early autumn
Cultivate	do not transplant seedlings, always sow where they are to grow, and thin; in the growing season, remove the flowers unless wanted for seed; it will self-sow but established plants can be divided in early spring
Harvest	strip leaves as they are needed from adult plants, but if the plants are grown from seed, wait until they are mature enough to produce flower-heads; dies down early winter, and starts to sprout again in late winter
History	sanguisorba comes from the Latin *sanguis*, blood and *sorbeo*, to check, and both this species and *S. officinalis* were used dried, as a styptic to stop bleeding, for which it was thought to be very effective; the Greek doctor, Dioscorides, included it in his book of medicinal plants, written in the 1st century A.D.

Burnet
flower and leaf

Burnet and cheese sandwich
In addition to its use as a salad ingredient, burnet gives an unusual and slightly strengthening flavour to cream cheese. A few leaves can make something special out of a sandwich.

Caraway

(Culinary) *Carum carvi*

Description	hardy biennial; flowers early or late summer; height 60cm (2ft)
Uses	the small, black narrow seeds are the seeds used in the seed-cake or caraway cake of Victorian days; they have a strong and distinctive flavour which overcomes other flavours and should be used sparingly with such dishes as baked apples, cheese, cabbage and soup. Caraway bread is still eaten in Germany, Sweden and Norway
Site/soil	a sunny place and light but fertile soil
Sow/plant	sow seed in early autumn or mid spring and thin to 30cm (1ft) apart
Cultivate	cover through winter in very wet weather – caraway grows badly in waterlogged or poorly drained soil; autumn-sown plants will flower the following summer, spring-sown ones in early summer the next year
Harvest	seeds when ripe in late summer or midsummer, depending on time of sowing; seeds will be black or dark brown, and the stems are cut and dried slowly until the seeds shake free
History	the Romans used caraway seed as a flavouring and in Shakespeare's Henry V Justice Shallow talks of a "last year's pippin, of my own graffing, with a dish of caraways". Caraway is used to flavour the liqueur Kummel, which is the German word for caraway

Caraway *plant*

Commercial caraway
Although caraway is a native of western Asia, it has been extensively cultivated in Europe, especially in the Netherlands. The seeds are not the only parts which can be eaten. The roots, boiled and dressed with parsley sauce, make an excellent dish.

Catmint, Catnip

(Culinary) *Nepeta cataria*

Description	ornamental; flowers midsummer–early autumn; height 30-60cm (1-2ft)
Uses	highly aromatic leaves and young shoots used to season soup, sauces and meat casseroles; small quantities of the fresh leaves can be added to salads, or used to rub over meat, rather in the way that garlic is used. Catmint tisane is said to help cure feverish colds
Site/soil	sun or shade, chalky or gravelly soil
Sow/plant	plant spring or autumn about 60cm (2ft) apart each way; it will grow from seed, but this is difficult to obtain
Cultivate	it is a native British plant and requires little care; remove the flowering stems before the buds open; if the plants are allowed to flower and then sheared over to about 23cm (9in) high when flowering has finished, they will flower again in early autumn
Harvest	strip leaves as required once the plants are well established, and use fresh for cooking
History	there is an old, anonymous saying: 'If you set it (catmint) the cats will eat it: if you sow it the cats won't know it'. It certainly has an extraordinary fascination for cats, and transplanted plants are likely to be completely destroyed unless protected for some weeks; by contrast, it is reputed to keep rats away. In Britain, catmint was used to make a mildly stimulating tea by those who could not afford the expensive imports from the Far East

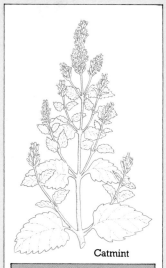

Catmint

Care of catmint
There are signs that catmint is regaining some of its earlier popularity as a border plant. Its grey-green foliage and spikes of purple flowers give it plenty of ornamental quality. Sometimes it is affected by powdery mildew; spray every 14 days with benomyl or dinocap.

Spray to cure mildew

Chamomile

(Medicinal, cosmetic) *Matricaria recutita*

Description	hardy herbaceous perennial; flowers late spring–mid autumn; low-growing but with flower stems about 30cm (1ft) tall
Uses	dried flowers of the double form used to make tea drunk after meals to help with digestion; an infusion of the flowers is said to lessen pain such as that of toothache, sore gums and throats, and can also be used as an eye bath; it is said to be strongly antiseptic. A rinse for lightening blonde hair can be made from 14g (½oz) of dried double flowers and ½l (1pt) of water boiled together for 20 minutes
Site/soil	sun, moist good loam; the single-flowered form needs sandy soil
Sow/plant	plant in early spring or autumn 45cm (1½ft) apart and firm-in well the small plants
Cultivate	keep clear of weeds while establishing by hand weeding, otherwise the small plants are easily harmed or hoed out
Harvest	cut the flowers when fully open, when dry, on a sunny day, so that they have their maximum content of essential oil, and dry quickly in single layers in warmth but not more than 35°C (95°F)
History	the bowling green on which Drake played his famous game is said to have been made of chamomile; the name comes from the old Greek, *chamaimelon*, literally, apple on the ground, referring to its odour when bruised or crushed

Chamomile *plant*

Chamomile lawns
The species *Anthemis nobilis* is the chamomile from which lawns are made. Planted on banks or paths it gives the herb garden an authentic fragrance. To make a lawn: clear the ground, remove stones and level the surface. Plant rooted pieces of chamomile at intervals of 10cm (4 in) in every direction.

Chamomile *detail*

Chervil

(Culinary) *Anthriscus cerefolium*

Chervil

Description	hardy biennial grown as an annual; flowers summer; height 45cm (1½ft)
Uses	leaves should be used fresh; their slightly sweet, aromatic flavour lends spice to fish dishes, cheese, chicken casseroles, mushrooms, and will make delicious soup or sauce; it is also one of the ingredients of *fines herbes;* it should be used fairly freely
Site/soil	some shade in summer, but sun in winter; any soil but not those that are badly drained and inclined to be wet
Sow/plant	sow seed in late summer for best germination, or in succession in spring, and summer, firm in by treading, and thin to 30cm (1ft) apart
Cultivate	remove flowers just before opening, and keep supplied with moisture
Harvest	take leaves from outside of plants, about 6 weeks after sowing and use fresh because it is difficult to dry successfully
History	chervil juice was much used in the Middle Ages as a blood-cleansing treatment and was probably introduced by the Romans; in 1573 Tusser listed it as one of the 'necessarie herbes to grow in the garden for physick'; Pliny thought that the seeds mixed in vinegar would cure hiccoughs, but this is one of the herbs that has always been more important as a flavouring agent in which rôle it has been used for thousands of years; Gerard records its use in a Dutch dish called 'Warmus'

Chervil soup
Break 3 eggs into a bowl and mix with 45ml (3 tablespoons) of chopped chervil. Bring 1 litre (1¾ pints) of chicken stock to boiling point and pour a little onto the egg. Stir the mixture vigorously and then pour it into the pan containing the rest of the stock. Stir it over gentle heat until the soup thickens. Do not let it boil. Season with salt, pepper and add a squeeze of lemon.

Chives

(Culinary) *Allium schoenoprasum*

Description	hardy bulbous perennial, dying down in autumn; flowers late spring–early summer; height 15-45cm (6-18in)
Uses	grass-like leaves, delicately flavoured with onion, are used fresh as a garnish to soups, sandwiches, salads and grilled chops or steak, mixed with cheese and egg dishes and as part of *fines herbes* and sauce tartare
Site/soil	sun or a little shade, most soils
Sow/plant	sow seed thinly in mid spring and thin to 15-30cm (6-12in) apart; plant in spring or autumn
Cultivate	keep free of weeds while seedlings; supply moisture in dry weather, otherwise they become infected with greenfly, and remove flowerheads; divide clumps every 3 years or so
Harvest	cut leaves as required when well established; cloches over plants in autumn will prolong the season, and start them growing again in late winter
History	chives have been included in British herb gardens since the 15th century and their cultivation has been traced back to the days of the Chinese in 3000 B.C.; the specific botanic name comes from two Greek words: *schoinos,* a rush and *orason*, a leek; Culpeper thought they were harmful, unless properly prepared by an 'alchymist' and then they could be used to help the flow of urine

Chives

Chives in pots
Chives can be grown quite successfully in pots, but they have a tendency to turn brown at the tips of the leaves, unless they are given a liquid feed every 14 days. Remember to remove the flower heads as soon as they form.

Comfrey, Knitbone

(Medicinal & culinary) *Symphytum officinale*

Comfrey

Description	hardy herbaceous perennial, dies down in autumn; flowers late spring–late summer; height 60-90cm (2-3ft)
Uses	comfrey leaves have considerable medicinal value, especially in skin complaints, for relieving sprains and bruises, and as a poultice for boils and abscesses; the roots are said to be helpful in the treatment of coughs and quinsy; the young leaves can be cooked and eaten like spinach
Site/soil	sun and most soils
Sow/plant	plant in spring or early–mid autumn, 60cm (2ft) apart each way
Cultivate	keep free of weeds, particularly grass, and mulch heavily every year in early spring and early summer with rotted organic matter; pieces of root can be detached and planted in spring to provide new plants, though plants can live for 20 years or more
Harvest	strip leaves as required in growing season
History	comfrey had a tremendous reputation in the Middle Ages for remedying broken bones, and it was grown as a matter of course in many cottage gardens to provide leaves for healing wounds; the name comfrey comes from *con firma*, alluding to the uniting of bones, and the Greek word *sympho*, means to unite; Culpeper recommended a decoction of crushed roots 'being outwardly applied, cure fresh wounds or cuts immediately'

The healing herb
Comfrey's reputation for healing damaged tissue once led to a belief that it could restore lost virginity. Recent research has not substantiated this claim. A poultice of grated comfrey root is, however, effective in healing sprains.

Coriander

(Culinary) *Coriandrum sativum*

Description	hardy annual; flowers early to mid-summer; height 23-30cm (9-12in)
Uses	the seeds are the part used, powdered in curry, sparingly in soup, sauces and marinades, and over pork, ham or veal, or sprinkled into cakes, biscuits and milk puddings; the odour is strong and unpleasant when unripe, but as the seeds ripen it becomes aromatic, even slightly sweet
Site/soil	sun and well-drained soil
Sow/plant	sow outdoors in mid spring, preferably in warm soil, or early autumn, and thin to 20-23cm (8-9in) apart
Cultivate	keep free of weeds especially when young, because coriander is a delicate plant, and protect from strong wind
Harvest	in late summer; the round seeds will lose their unpleasant smell when ripe and will be yellowish-brown
History	the name Coriandrum is derived from the Greek *koros,* bed bug, and refers to the disagreeable smell of the leaves and unripe seeds. The ripe seeds, tasting of lemon and sage and coated with sugar, were once very popular as a sweetmeat; the chinese thought the seeds had the power of conferring immortality; coriander seeds have been found in ancient Egyptian tombs and were once in general use for flavouring wine, preserves and meats

Coriander *plant*

To aid digestion
Coriander has long been used to treat and prevent various disorders of the stomach. The seeds contain a volatile oil which acts against flatulence. An infusion can be made by pouring boiling water over a handful of crushed seeds.

Costmary, Alecost, Mace

(Culinary) *Chrysanthemum balsamita*

Description	hardy, long-lived herbaceous perennial, dies down almost completely in autumn; flowers late summer–early autumn; spreading flower stems 60-120cm (2-4ft) in height
Uses	the sweetly scented, dried leaves, rather like camphor in their aroma, can be used amongst clothes and household linen, like lavender; use sparingly in salads, soups and stuffings; the dried leaves retain their fragrance for long periods
Site/soil	a warm sunny place and a dryish soil
Sow/plant	plant in mid spring or early–mid autumn about 60cm (2ft) apart
Cultivate	easily grown in the above conditions, it will spread quite quickly and should be dug up and divided every 3 years or so, replanting at once; grown in shade, it does not flower, but becomes very leafy
Harvest	strip leaves after the middle of early summer and dry quickly but not with too much warmth because they are delicate
History	the leaves were used to flavour beer before hops became the standard ingredient; they were also used by the Elizabethans for perfuming water and strewing floors. Costmary was considered to be effective in the cure of dysentery, having antiseptic properties. The 'blade of mace' referred to in many old recipes is in fact a leaf of costmary and not the oriental spice

Costmary *plant*

An untidy plant
Costmary is interesting chiefly for its historical uses rather than its present value, or its ornamental contribution to the garden. In fact, it is a very untidy, straggling sort of plant and has never been particularly popular with gardeners.

Dill

(Culinary, medicinal) *Anethum graveolens*

Description	hardy annual; flowers early–late summer; height 60-90cm (2-3ft)
Uses	fresh leaves used to flavour fish dishes, salads, bland vegetables, egg and cheese recipes; slightly bitter seeds are suitable for soups, strongly-flavoured vegetables, and mixed with sauces or herb butters. Dill seed tea is supposed to stop an attack of hiccoughs, remove bad breath and be mildly sleep-inducing
Site/soil	sunny, with a moist, but not waterlogged soil
Sow/plant	sow seed in early to mid spring, and thin to about 23cm (9in) apart; also in midsummer for an autumn supply
Cultivate	do not transplant; keep well watered to prevent premature flowering and therefore an end to the plant, and also avoid greenfly infestation; plants will self-sow, producing stronger specimens
Harvest	strip leaves as required after early summer; seeds should be taken as they begin to change to brown in late summer, because they fall rapidly once ripe, and are easily lost
History	the name comes from the Norse word *dilla*, meaning to lull, as it was once considered a cure for sleeplessness, the seeds being given to babies to soothe them; seeds were also nibbled during Lent to dull the pangs of hunger; oil of dill is still used to prepare gripewater

Dill *plant*

The fish herb
Dill is unusual in that the leaves can be used as a herb and the seeds as a spice. Both are widely used – especially in fish dishes. The seeds have an important commercial use in the making of dill vinegar which is used for pickling.

Elder

(Culinary, medicinal) *Sambucus nigra*

Description	hardy large shrub or small tree; flowers midsummer; height 1½-3m (5-10ft), spread 3-6m (10-20ft)
Uses	fresh flowers and berries make excellent white, still or sparkling wine; flowers can be added to jams and jellies, or milk puddings, or made into fritters; dried flowers are used for tisane or tea, elderflower water is said to be good for the eyes or as a skin cleansing lotion
Site/soil	sun or shade, any soil
Sow/plant	plant in autumn or sow seed in spring; one plant is generally sufficient
Cultivate	it is easily grown and no special cultivation is required; elderberry grows rapidly and needs moderate pruning in early spring to keep it under control; seeds from the berries germinate readily, or root division in spring or autumn can be used for increase
Harvest	flowers in midsummer; berries when ripe and fully black, in late summer–early autumn
History	a much used herb, steeped in tradition since Anglo-Saxon times when it was called Eldrun, from *oeld*; it is said that the Cross of Calvary was made of it, and that Judas hanged himself on a gallows of elder; cutting it is said to bring bad luck, but planting it outside the main door of the home wards off witches and evil influences; in the 17th century the leaves were fixed to the outside of doors and windows on the last day of April for the same purpose

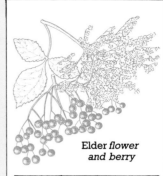

Elder *flower and berry*

Elderflower cup
Take the peel of two lemons and put into a jug with 112g (4 oz) of sugar and 8 heads of elderflower, freshly gathered. Pour into the jug 600ml (1 pint) of boiling water and stir until the sugar has dissolved. Cover, then leave to cool. When the drink is cold, strain it through muslin and serve it diluted with water and ice. There are many variations on this drink, including one in which a mild fermentation is started in order to produce a 'fizz'.

Eyebright

(Medicinal) *Euphrasia officinalis*

Description	hardy annual; flowers midsummer–early autumn; height 5-20cm (2-8in)
Uses	as an eye lotion, the whole plant being used when in flower and infused in water, to relieve soreness and inflammation, weakness of the eyes and other sight disorders
Site/soil	a native British plant; a sunny or slightly shady position and any well-drained soil, preferably chalky
Sow/plant	sow seed in spring and thin to about 10cm (4in) apart
Cultivate	no special cultivation is required except to keep the seedlings free of weeds; once established, grass should be allowed to grow amongst it because its roots are slightly parasitic on the roots of the grass; it will seed from year to year amongst the grass
Harvest	pull up the plant complete with flowers in mid–late summer and use fresh
History	euphrasia is derived from the Greek *Euphrosyne,* meaning gladness, i.e. gladness that the sight of the eyes was improved or restored; Gerard said 'It is very much commended for the eyes ... the juice thereof mixed with white Wine and dropped into the eyes, taketh away the darkness and dimnesse of the eyes'. Culpeper confirms that used in the same way it 'helped all infirmities of the eyes that cause dimness of sight', but it did not prevent the poet Milton from losing his sight

Eyebright *plant*

To make an eye compress
Boil 56g (2oz) of chopped, dried eyebright in 500ml (0.9 pint) for two minutes. Leave the infusion to stand for 30 minutes. Strain. Soak a doubled piece of lint, and apply the compress for 15 to 20 minutes.

Fennel
(Culinary) *Foeniculum vulgare*

Description	hardy herbaceous perennial, dies down mid–late autumn; flowers midsummer; height 60cm (2ft), spread 1½-2m (5-7ft)
Uses	feathery leaves have an aromatic, aniseed flavour, and go well with all fish dishes, pork, veal, soup and salad dressings; seeds have stronger flavour and are used in pickling cucumbers and gherkins, and with sauerkraut
Site/soil	sun or light shade, shelter and a moist and chalky soil
Sow/plant	sow seed in mid–late spring, preferably in soil which is warming up, and thin to 45cm (1½ft) apart
Cultivate	keep weeds under control and remove flowering stems before the flower, unless seeds are needed; do not grow near dill, as the resultant hybrid seeds will produce neither fennel nor dill plants
Harvest	take leaves when they are wanted at any time from mature plants, and from seed-grown plants, after early summer; seeds are collected when still light green, after early autumn, and dried in a low temperature
History	in the Middle Ages, fennel was hung over doors on Midsummer's Eve to ward off witchcraft and evil spirits; a common ingredient of Anglo-Saxon recipes, the seeds are still included in the British Pharmaceutical Index as a cure for flatulence; it was cultivated by the Romans for culinary and medicinal uses

Fennel *plant*

Fennel hand cream
Make an infusion with 15ml (1 tablespoon) of fennel and 100ml (3.5 fl oz) of water. Strain when cool. Warm together 10ml (2 teaspoons) arrowroot, 30ml (2 tablespoons) glycerine, 30ml (2 tablespoons) lavender water and the infusion until the mixture thoroughly blended.

Garlic

(Culinary, medicinal) *Allium sativum*

Description	bulbous plant, hardy except in severe cold; flowers early–midsummer; height 60-75cm (2-2½ft)
Uses	cloves used to flavour more or less any savoury recipe, in particular meat casseroles, salads, grilled meats and kebabs, and rice dishes; said to have an antiseptic effect, to help digestion and to cleanse the blood
Site/soil	sunny, preferably sheltered, well-drained but fertile soil
Sow/plant	plant cloves in early–mid autumn or early spring 5cm (2in) deep and 15cm (6in) apart, 30cm (1ft) between rows; choose the largest cloves
Cultivate	feed autumn-planted cloves in early spring with a nitrogenous fertilizer and in early summer supply a dressing of sulphate of potash; feed spring-planted garlic with sulphate of potash in midsummer, both dressings at about 14-28g per sq m (½-1oz per sq yd); keep clear of weeds at all times and remove the flowers; support stems with a stake behind each plant
Harvest	late summer–early autumn when tops have turned yellow, by digging out the bulbs; clean bulbs, leave to dry in sun, and then store by hanging in a dry, dark, cool place
History	the name comes from the Anglo-Saxon *gar*, a spear and *leac*, meaning leek, since it is a member of the leek tribe with a spear-shaped leaf

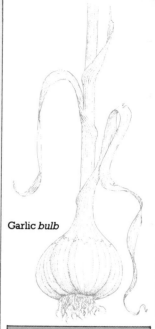

Garlic *bulb*

The magical clove
Many civilisations have attributed magical and miraculous properties to Garlic. The ancient Egyptians used it to ward off disease and evil spirits and to discover the fertility of women. The Greeks, on the other hand, believed that it could inhibit magic.

Gentian, yellow

(Medicinal) *Gentiana lutea*

Description	ornamental, hardy herbaceous perennial; flowers early–midsummer; height 90-120cm (3-4ft)
Uses	the intensely bitter roots have been used, dried, in the treatment of jaundice, also as a tonic to improve appetite, and to alleviate dyspeptic conditions; it has always been considered of great use in the treatment of many stomach disorders and the juice of the roots is an ingredient of many medicinal 'bitters'
Site/soil	sun and shelter, and a moist, deep, rich soil
Sow/plant	plant early–mid autumn, or spring, 60cm (2ft) apart; sow seed in a shallow pot or pan in early spring, prick out, and plant in late spring or early autumn
Cultivate	keep clear of weeds, water well in dry weather, and mulch every year in late spring with rotted organic matter; seed-grown plants take 3 years to flower; divide established plants every 3 years or so, in early spring
Harvest	dig up in autumn, and dry roots and creeping underground stems slowly
History	the name gentian refers to the King of Illyria (180-167 B.C.), whose name was Gentius, and who is thought, according to Dioscorides, to have discovered that gentians had the property of suppressing fevers. Gentian wine was a popular aperitif in 18th century England and the plant was widely prescribed in North American herbal medicine in the 19th century

Gentian *flowers*

The bitter herb
Gentian is still considered to be the best provider of 'bitters' for aperitifs and alcoholic drinks. The reason for this is that the essential ingredient, glycoside gentiopicrin, can be extracted with alcohol. The roots can grow to the thickness of a man's arm, and in the districts where the plant is grown commercially, special tools are used to dig them out.

Honeysuckle

(Medicinal) *Lonicera periclymenum*

Description	ornamental, hardy climber; flowers early summer–early autumn; height 3-4½m (10-15ft), spread 2m (6ft)
Uses	leaves are said to be useful as part of a gargle for sore throats and in treating liver complaints; a syrup of the flowers has been used to treat asthma and other respiratory troubles, and distilled flower water to alleviate nervous headaches
Site/soil	shade for the roots and some of the top growth; any soil, preferably chalky
Sow/plant	plant autumn–spring about 180cm (6ft) apart
Cultivate	supply supports for the twining stems at least 3m (10ft) high; keep well watered in hot, dry weather, and mulch every year in late spring with rotted organic matter; prune to restrict if required, in early spring; increase by layering in late summer, or by semi-ripe cuttings in mid–late summer
History	Culpeper described honeysuckle as a 'hot martial plant in the sign of Cancer' – and said that 'the oil made by the infusion of the leaves is good for the cramp and convulsions of the nerves'. It was named after Adam Lonicer, born 1528, a physician and naturalist who wrote a new natural history which contained a good deal of unusual and interesting facts about plants; although the exotic fragrance of honeysuckle has led to its being grown largely as an ornamental, it is still used medicinally in many countries

Honeysuckle *plant*

Home antiseptic
Honeysuckle contains a number of antibiotic substances and a good deal of salicylic acid – a substance used in many medicines. An infusion of the flowers is known to be effective in treating bronchial complaints and coughs.

Honeysuckle *flower*

Hops

(Culinary and medicinal) *Humulus lupulus*

Hop *flowers and leaf*

Description	hardy climber, dies down in autumn; flowers late summer–early autumn; height 3-4½m (10-15ft), spread 1m (3ft)
Uses	dried female flowers used to give bitter flavour to beer; an infusion of dried hops 'expels urine', to quote a 17th century herbalist; the essential ingredient, lupulin, has considerable medicinal value for soothing, helping with sleeplessness, and improving the digestion
Site/soil	sun and shelter from cold wind, deep moist, fertile soil
Sow/plant	sow seed outdoors in spring and thin to a final spacing of 120-150cm (4-5ft) apart; plant mid autumn or early spring at same spacing
Cultivate	supply supports for the twining stems at least 3m (10ft) tall; water heavily in dry weather, and mulch in early spring with rotted organic matter; cut down the twining shoots in mid autumn
Harvest	strip female hop cones in early autumn when yellowish-brown, and dry at once
History	hops have been used in Bavarian beers since the 11th century and in British beers since the 1520s; young hop shoots were boiled and served to be eaten like asparagus, and are still, in some country districts; the word hop comes from the Anglo-Saxon *hoppan*, meaning to climb; hops are sometimes grown as ornamental climbers

The brewer's herb
The part of the plant used in beer making is the pale yellow, cone-shaped flower which is coated in a bitter, resinous dust called *lupulin*. It is this substance which gives hop beers their characteristic flavours.

Horseradish

(Culinary) *Armoracia rusticana*

Description	hardy perennial; flowers midsummer; height 60cm (2ft)
Uses	hot, peppery-flavoured roots are mixed with cream to make a sauce used with roast beef, trout, sausages and ham, it contains natural antibiotics and is an aid to digestion
Site/soil	any site and soil, but the latter preferably deep and moist
Sow/plant	plant root cuttings 7.5cm (3in) long in early spring, 30cm (1ft) apart, just covered with soil; for best results dig trenches 60cm (2ft) deep; fill with topsoil 30cm (1ft) deep, then add 10cm (4in) of rotted organic matter, and then the rest of the soil; make the bed some distance away from cultivated plants, because horseradish is strong growing and could quickly swamp them
Cultivate	remove the sideshoots and flowers as they appear; dig up completely in autumn, as the quality of the roots declines rapidly, and replant
Harvest	keep the largest and thickest roots, clean them, tie in bundles and store in sand through the winter; for replanting, use those which are of pencil thickness, and at least 20cm (8in) long
History	used in Germany in the 1500s as a substitute for mustard and in Britain in Pepy's time as a flavouring for beer; it was once used as an antidote to scurvy, as an emetic, and applied bruised to chilbains

Horseradish *root and leaves*

Horseradish sauce
Grate 2 tablespoons of horseradish root (fine or coarse according to taste) and add it gradually to 300ml (½ pint) of cream, or soured cream, until the required consistency and strength is reached. Add salt and black pepper. Serve with roast beef or smoked fish.

Hyssop

(Culinary, medicinal) *Hyssopus officinalis*

Description	ornamental, almost evergreen sub-shrub; flowers early summer–mid autumn, pink or white, as well as blue; height 30-60cm (2-3ft)
Uses	aromatic leaves need to be used sparingly with salads, game and stews; they help in the digestion of fatty meats; hyssop tea is said to be excellent for relieving coughs and catarrh, and the fresh green leaves and shoot tops, infused, are still used to relieve rheumatism
Site/soil	sunny and sheltered, well-drained, preferably chalky soil
Sow/plant	plant in early–mid autumn, or mid spring, 60cm (2ft) apart or sow seed outdoors in mid spring, and thin gradually to the same spacing
Cultivate	keep clear of weeds while young; renew plants every 4 years or so from semi-ripe cuttings taken in late summer; plant in their permanent positions the following spring
Harvest	strip leaves as required once established; cut flowers just as they are fully open, unless required for ornament
History	a popular plant for edging the knot gardens of Elizabethan times, hyssop was used in very ancient days as a cleansing herb for sacred places; it was formerly much used medicinally for a variety of respiratory complaints, and grown in monastery gardens as a bee plant. It is said to be one of the herbs used in the original, if not the modern, recipe for making Chartreuse liqueur

Hyssop *plant*

Knot gardens
Hyssop, when clipped can be used as an edging for a traditional knot garden.

Iris, Orris Root

(Cosmetic) *Iris florentina, Iris foetidissima*

Description	ornamental, hardy rhizomatous perennials; flower late spring–early summer; height: *Iris florentina* 90-120cm (3-4ft), *Iris foetidissima* 60-75cm (2-2½ft)
Uses	*I. florentina*, Orris root, used dried and powdered as a fixative in perfumes; its violet fragrance ensures that it is used as a base for nearly all such perfumes; also added to many cosmetics and potpourris; roots of *I. foetidissima* are still occasionally prescribed, in powdered form, to relieve pain, cramp and convulsions
Site/soil	sun and good drainage of soil are important, with some chalk present
Sow/plant	plant in mid spring, 60cm (2ft) apart, with the fleshy rhizome (creeping underground stem) only half buried; mix bonemeal into the soil a week before planting at 90g per sq m (3oz per sq yd)
Cultivate	keep soil moist while rhizomes establish; remove seedheads unless they are wanted for decoration; feed with superphosphate at 30g per sq m (1 oz per sq yd) annually in mid spring; dig up in midsummer every 4th year, divide and replant the young sections of rhizomes
Harvest	roots, when plant is mature at 3 years, after flowering
History	Iris remains have been found in Egyptian tombs, and the plant was named after the Iris in Greek mythology, the deity of the rainbow

Iris *flower and* Orris root

Iris florentina
The Florentine iris, the plant from which orris root is obtained, is still grown commercially in northern Italy, but its most important use is in the making of toothpaste and toilet preparations. The root, when lifted, has little scent. But, as it dries, it begins to take on a scent of violets.

Lavender

(Cosmetic, medicinal) *Lavandula officinalis*

Description	ornamental hardy evergreen shrub; flowers midsummer; height 60-90cm (2-3ft)
Uses	fragrant flowers can be dried and used for potpourri, perfume and violet-water, sachets, pillows and cushions; lavender tea made from the leaves and shoot tips has some effect in relieving nervous headaches, provided it is drunk in moderation; oil of lavender rubbed on the skin wards off insects
Site/soil	sun and shelter, well-drained light soil
Sow/plant	plant mid spring or early autumn 60cm (2ft) apart
Cultivate	clip early–mid spring, so as to remove all but 2.5-5cm (1-2in) of last year's growth, and do this annually, otherwise plants get very leggy. Replace every few years or so, using cuttings taken and rooted any time in mid–late summer after flowering
Harvest	gather flower-spikes for drying when just coming into bloom, and for distilling about a week later
History	lavender was grown commercially in Mitcham, near London, only 100 years ago, on such a scale that there were 300 acres of it. In Gerard's Herbal, he recommends that lavender will 'profiteth them much that have the palsie, if they be washed with the distilled water of the floures'. In the early 1600s, Charles I granted a monopoly of soap making to one William Yardley who perfumed his soaps with lavender

Lavender *plant*

Ornamental uses
Lavender is grown chiefly for its purple flowers and its scent. In herb gardens, it can be used as an edging shrub because it will put up with fairly ruthless clipping.

Lavender *flower and leaf*

Lovage

(Culinary) *Levisticum officinale*

Description	hardy perennial, dying down in autumn; flowers early–late summer; height 90cm (3ft)
Uses	leaves used fresh or dried, have strong celery flavour, and can be added to a great variety of savoury dishes, especially salads, soups and casseroles; the flavour improves with cooking; the seeds also can be used in casseroles, meat pies and with game
Site/soil	sun or some shade, deep moist soils but not heavy clay
Sow/plant	sow seeds outdoors in late summer, and transplant the following spring to 120cm (4ft) apart, however, one plant is usually ample for a family
Cultivate	mulch in mid spring every year, with rotted organic matter and water well in dry, hot weather; remove flowering stems unless seed is wanted; increase every few years by root division in spring; each piece should have an 'eye' or bud and be buried 5cm (2in) deep
Harvest	take leaves from adult plants as needed and use fresh, or dry for winter use
History	the common name is possibly derived from 'love-ache', the name used for it 5 centuries ago – a corrupt form of levisticum, itself a corruption of Ligisticum, from Liguria in Italy; Lovage is much used in Italian cookery, and is part of the yeast extract Maggi. A West of England drink called lovage cordial was once very popular and was sold by public houses

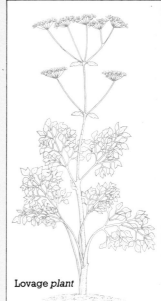

Lovage *plant*

A complete herb
Lovage is one of the most underrated herbs, being a very striking ornamental plant as well as an extremely useful one. All parts of the plant can be used for culinary purposes, including the stems which can be candied like Angelica. It can also be used for scenting baths and is known to possess some antiseptic properties.

Marigold

(Culinary, medicinal) *Calendula officinalis*

Description	hardy annual; flowers summer–mid autumn; height 30cm (12in)
Uses	the flower is the part chiefly used, the petals having a distinctive flavour; they can take the place of saffron for colouring many foods, e.g. rice, omelettes, soups, custards, puddings and cakes; the leaves can be used shredded in salads. Dried petals have been used in treating of chronic ulcer, the removal of scars, and the quicker healing of wounds
Site/soil	any soil and a sunny position
Sow/plant	sow outdoors mid spring and thin to 30cm (12in) apart
Cultivate	Keep clear of weeds while young, and remove flower-heads unless you want self-sown seedlings, which will tend to throw up orange, single-flowered plants
Harvest	pull the petals from the flowers when just fully expanded, and dry quickly in the shade, preferably in single layers; strip leaves during dry, fine conditions
History	in 1373, marigolds were referred to as Seint Mary Gouldes and, in 1526, the *Grete Herbal* named the plants as Mary gowles or ruddes. Marigolds are an ancient holy flower of Indian Buddhists, but in Western Europe they had a more plebian use, because the petals were once stocked by the barrelful by shopkeepers for various uses, such as hair dyeing, or colouring butter and cheese

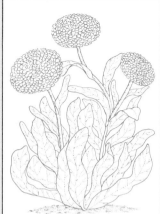

Marigold *plant in flower*

Tired feet
An infusion made from fresh leaves of marigolds is said to be very effective as a soothing footbath. Remember to crush the leaves before pouring on the boiling water – and let it cool before putting your feet in!

73

Marjoram

(Culinary) *Origanum majorana, O. onites,*

Description	*sweet marjoram,* half-hardy annual, flowers midsummer–early autumn; height 20cm (8in); *pot* and *wild marjoram,* perennials; flowering midsummer–mid autumn; height 60cm (2ft)
Uses	sweet and unusual aroma to the leaves, which are used in the same way as thyme, which they can replace in stuffings, or with pork, veal, omelettes and bouquet garni
Site/soil	sweet or knotted marjoram needs sun, warmth and a well-drained, but fertile, soil; pot marjoram and wild marjoram (oregano) will be happy with sun and light, dryish soil
Sow/plant	sow seed of sweet marjoram indoors in warmth in early–mid spring, prick out and finally plant out at the end of late spring after hardening off, spaced at 20cm (8in) intervals; protect from late frosts. Plant pot marjoram and wild marjoram outdoors in mid spring, about 30cm (12in) apart
Cultivate	shade sweet marjoram until established and weed well when young, as it is slow to grow; water in dry weather; pot and wild marjoram can be left to their own devices, but should be protected with deep mulches through the winter; pot marjoram can be dug up in early autumn, cut down and put into pots, when it will sprout fresh growth
Harvest	strip leaves from all marjorams for drying just before the flowers start to show through the 'knots'; its aroma is stronger when dried; for general use, remove the leaves as required and use fresh

Marjoram *plant*

The game herb
Throughout history, marjoram has been used with game and strong meats. Largely due to the fact that it is one of the most strongly flavoured of herbs. Use fresh leaves whenever possible.

Mint

(Culinary) *Mentha spp*

Description	hardy perennials, dying down in autumn; flowering mostly mid to late summer; height from 20-90cm (8in-3ft)
Uses	fresh leaves of garden mint *(Mentha spicata)* can be used with new potatoes, peas, beans, salads, for mint sauce, stuffings, bouquet garni, in summer drinks, and jellies. Pepper mint *(M. piperita)* has excellent digestive properties; pineapple mint, apple mint and also Eau de Cologne mint (with purplish tinted leaves), should be used sparingly in teas, summer drinks, fruit salads and ice creams
Site/soil	any site and soil, though a moist one is preferred; pineapple mint needs good drainage
Sow/plant	plant spring or autumn where roots can be confined, about 30cm (12in) apart; plant pineapple mint in spring only
Cultivate	prevent encroaching on other cultivated plants; increase by digging up rooted pieces of stems and replanting at any time during spring or autumn; protect pineapple mint through winter with a cloche
Harvest	strip fresh leaves as required for use; for drying, remove whole shoots and avoid bruising as much as possible, otherwise the aroma is lost
History	used for sauces in the 3rd century A.D. and for cleaning teeth in the 6th century; Gerard recommended its application 'with salt to the bitings of mad dogs'

Mint *plant*

Invasive mint
Mint will grow well almost anywhere. If it is near water, or in moist soil, it will grow very quickly. Unfortunately, it also spreads rapidly and must be contained if it is not to become a weed. Nevertheless, it is one of the most useful of herbs to keep in the kitchen garden.

Mint *leaf*

Nasturtium

(Culinary) *Tropaeolum majus*

Description	half-hardy annual, trailing or climbing; flowers early summer–mid autumn; height 180cm (6ft), bush variety 30cm (1ft)
Uses	peppery-flavoured leaves can be used in salads, and chopped, in sandwiches and cream cheeses, but should be added to these only at the last minute, otherwise the cheese becomes unpleasant-tasting; they have some antibiotic properties; the pickled young seeds will substitute adequately for capers
Site/soil	sun and a poor well-drained soil
Sow/plant	sow seed 30cm (12in) apart in mid–late spring
Cultivate	protect seeds and seedlings from frost, and supply supports for the climbing kinds to twine up; spray blackfly with bioresemethrin; it will self-seed in warm places
Harvest	strip leaves as required; highest vitamin C content is present just before flowering
History	nasturtium leaves and flowers were once much used in cookery from the time of its introduction in 1580, when it was known as Indian Cress; the use of the petals and leaves in salads comes from the Orient, and there is a Turkish recipe of 1862 for salad made from the flowers; a recipe of 1739 for pickling the seeds advises 'gather your little knobs, put them in cold water and salt for three days...' Water cress, once described as *Nasturtium officinale,* is not related to this plant, although the leaves are said to resemble cress in flavour.

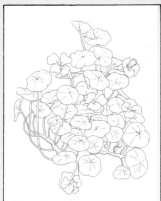

Nasturtium *plant*

The flower of love
This was the name given to nasturtium by one Professor Binet who claimed that it was an effective aphrodisiac and rejuvenator.

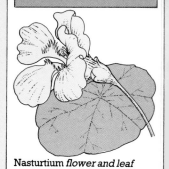

Nasturtium *flower and leaf*

Parsley

(Culinary) *Petroselinum crispum*

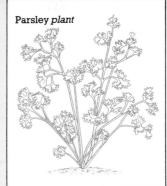

Parsley *plant*

Description	hardy biennial grown as an annual, French parsley has plain leaves and stronger flavour; flowers midsummer; height 15-30cm (6-12in)
Uses	fresh leaves can be chopped and used as a garnish for a variety of savoury dishes, in sauces, sandwiches and salads; in bouquet garni and fines herbes, and as the basis for maître d'hotel butter
Site/soil	sun or a little shade; moist, deep, fertile soil
Sow/plant	sow seed thinly outdoors in mid spring; the warmer the soil the quicker the germination, which can take 10-35 days, and thin to 23cm (9in) apart; sow also early in midsummer to provide fresh leaves for winter use
Cultivate	keep free of weeds while young, watch for slugs, and water well in dry weather to prevent invasion by greenfly; protect winter crop with cloches; for pot cultivation, grow one plant to a 12cm (5in) pot and use a good potting compost
Harvest	strip leaves as required after early summer; they have their highest vitamin C content when fresh; for drying, cut in summer and dry rapidly to retain colour and aroma
History	Parsley's reputation for slow germination is said to be because it has to go down to the Devil and back seven times before sprouting; the ancient Greeks used it for making wreaths for the dead and chaplets for victors in sport, and it was dedicated to Persephone

The miracle worker
Parsley is one of those herbs that has been credited with the curing and prevention of practically everything. It was also believed, during the Middle Ages, to bring the most appalling luck. It does have great value, however, being rich in iron, calcium, and vitamin C.

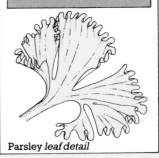

Parsley *leaf detail*

Pennyroyal

(Medicinal) *Mentha pulegium*

Description	hardy perennial, dying down in autumn, low-growing and mat-forming, flowers mid–late summer
Uses	pungently-flavoured leaves can be used sparingly in stuffings, sausages, cream cheeses, dumplings and toppings for casseroles; pennyroyal tea is said to be helpful for flatulence, and nausea, and has been used as a remedy by country people for colds and coughs
Site/soil	sun or a little shade, moist sandy soil
Sow/plant	plant in spring or autumn spaced 23cm (9in) apart each way
Cultivate	keep well watered at all times, because it is found naturally at the sides of pools or on heaths with underground streams; protect in winter against severe cold, and put some plants into 13cm (5in) pans in autumn as an insurance, and keep under cover; increase by dividing existing plants in early autumn or spring
Harvest	strip fresh leaves as required from early summer onwards, or remove leaves for drying for tea just before flowering
History	much used medicinally in the past; Pliny said that a chaplet of pennyroyal would relieve giddiness, and headache. Anglo Saxon medical works referred to it frequently, and it was commonly thought to purify drinking water

Pennyroyal *plant*

The sailors herb
Pennyroyal, it is said, was taken to sea by sailors so that they could purify their drinking water with it. But it may also have had something to do with the fact that this herb is widely reputed to ward off vermin.

Pennyroyal *leaf detail*

Purslane

(Culinary) *Portulaca oleracea*

Description	half-hardy annual; flowers early–midsummer; there is also a yellow-leaved form; height 15cm (6in)
Uses	leaves and young tender shoots are used in salads; the older leaves can be boiled and eaten like spinach, or mixed with sorrel to make soup; stems are sometimes pickled for winter salads; seeds also are occasionally used for flavouring
Site/soil	shelter and sun, with a freely-draining soil
Sow/plant	sow seeds in gentle warmth in mid spring; plant out after hardening off in late spring, 30cm (12in) apart; sow twice more at 2-week intervals to obtain a succession through the summer
Cultivate	keep well supplied with water in dry weather; purslane is a thirsty plant; remove flowering stems unless seeds are wanted
Harvest	take leaves when young plants are well established, in about six weeks; stripping, except for the central shoot, will encourage a fresh crop of leaves; seeds can be taken from the first batch of plants
History	purslane is a very old herb and one which originated in the tropics; it has been used all over the world since the very earliest times; it had a good deal of medicinal use originally, chewing the leaves was said to take away toothache and, mixed with oil of roses, to alleviate sore mouths and gums

Purslane *plant*

Dutch favourite
Purslane is extensively cultivated in the Netherlands as a salad crop and appears in the Dutch Pharmacopoeia of 1747 as a remedy for inflammation of the bladder and piles. Pickled purslane was known during the 14th Century, but as a salad plant it may be much older than that.

Purslane *leaf detail*

Roses

(Culinary, cosmetic) *Rosa spp.*

Description	ornamental hardy deciduous shrubs; flower early–late summer; height 120-180cm (4-6ft), spread 90-150cm (3-5ft)
Uses	hips of *R. canina* (dog-rose), *R. rugosa* and *R. rubiginosa* (sweetbriar) contain large quantities of vitamin C and a good deal of vitamin A; they can be made into tea, syrup, purée and jelly; petals of these and other species can be added to crabapple jelly, and candied; petals of *R. damascena* are used in potpourri, and for making Attar of Roses
Site/soil	sun, shelter, and well-drained fertile soil
Sow/plant	plant autumn–spring at 120-180cm (4-6ft) spacing each way
Cultivate	keep watered if the weather is dry after planting; mulch with rotted garden compost or similar material in late spring every year; no pruning needed except to keep within space available, and to remove dead, old or diseased shoots and branches; increase from hardwood cuttings in mid autumn
Harvest	collect hips when bright red or crimson in mid autumn; for immediate use they should be slightly soft, but for drying they should be firm; petals for perfumery use should be stripped early in the morning of a dry day
History	the Romans covered the floors of their banqueting-halls with rose petals, and thought the roots had a salutary effect on hydrophobia, one of the symptoms of rabies, hence the name *Rosa canina*

Dog rose *flower*

Rose hips
Unlike many herbs, rose hips have a proven record of medicinal value. They are rich in vitamin C and are very effective in the treatment of diarrhoea. The seeds, or *achenes*, are good for kidney stones and colic. The down which surrounds the seeds is a known cure for worms.

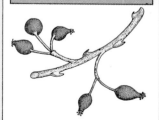

Rose hips

Rosemary

(Culinary, medicinal) *Rosmarinus officinalis*

Description	ornamental, more or less hardy evergreen shrub; flowers late spring; height 90-150cm (3-5ft)
Uses	fresh leaves have a penetrating and pleasing aroma, and are used with lamb, pork, veal and rabbit or, sparingly, with chicken, mushrooms, eggs and cheese dishes; sprigs can be added to oil to make oil of rosemary; leaves will make a diuretic tea and can be used to form part of hair rinses and tonics
Site/soil	full sun and a well-drained, dry soil
Sow/plant	mid-late spring; one plant is sufficient
Cultivate	keep protected from cold wind while establishing; prune to keep within the space available after flowering; increase from tip or half-ripe cuttings taken mid–late summer and planted the following spring; a severely cold winter will kill rosemary
Harvest	strip leaves or shoots at any time
History	rosemary's penetrating aroma can be felt trickling up through the nose to the top of the forehead, and perhaps because of this the Greek students twined it in their hair at examination times to help them remember; hence also Shakespeare's; 'There's rosemary, that's for remembrance'. The name comes from the Latin *ros*, dew and *maris*, sea – it grows naturally near the sea. It was thought to be a disinfectant, even against the Plague, and was used to keep clothing free of moths

Rosemary *leaf detail*

Love tokens
The Romans associated rosemary with prosperity and fertility and gave it to brides and bridegrooms at weddings.

Rue, Herb of Grace

(Culinary, medicinal) *Ruta graveolens*

Description	ornamental, hardy evergreen shrub; flowers mid–late summer; blue-grey-leaved form is *R. graveolens* 'Jackman's Blue; height 60-90cm (2-3ft)
Uses	bitter-tasting fresh leaves can be used, with discretion, in pickles, salads, sandwiches and meat casseroles; it has also been recommended, in modern times, for coughs, croup and bronchitis
Site/soil	a sunny place, and well-drained poor soil
Sow/plant	sow seed outdoors thinly in mid spring, and thin to 45cm (18in) intervals; plant in mid spring or early autumn at the same spacing
Cultivate	rue is particularly easily grown and needs no attention once the seedlings have taken hold; in sunless places it becomes leggy, and in severely cold winters will be killed; cuttings taken in mid–late spring root easily and quickly outdoors in a shaded place, they can be planted in their permanent position when well rooted
Harvest	strip leaves to use fresh, when needed; for drying, remove just before flowering; dried leaves are less pungent
History	ruta comes from the Greek *rueo,* to set free, because it was thought to cure so many diseases; it was also considered to have the power of endowing second sight, a property perhaps confused with another from Pliny's time, when painters ate a great deal to preserve and sharpen their normal eyesight

Rue *plant*

The complete antidote
Rue, more than any other plant, gained a reputation in ancient times for its anti-toxin effects and its ability to ward off venomous creatures. Traces of these beliefs can still be found in Italy and the Netherlands. In recent times, the plant has been used in the treatment of weakened blood-vessels.

Rue *leaf detail*

Sage

(Culinary) *Salvia officinalis*

Description	ornamental, more or less hardy evergreen shrub, several cultivars with leaves variously coloured; flowers midsummer; height 60-75cm (2-2½ft)
Uses	fresh leaves have a highly aromatic, sharp flavour which goes well with pork, duck, goose, venison, veal and hare; also use in sausages, hamburgers, stuffings and bouquet garni, and wrapped round eels
Site/soil	preferably sunny, with medium-light soil on the chalky side
Sow/plant	sow seed thinly in a cold frame in early–mid spring, prick out into individual pots and plant as soon as the pots are full of root; also plant in mid spring; space all 45cm (18in) apart
Cultivate	trim over after flowering to encourage bushy growth, but do not cut so far down that shoots older than the current season's are pruned, otherwise new growth will be weak and poor; replace every 4 or 5 years, and protect in severely cold winters; soft or semi-ripe cuttings taken in summer root readily, but the stems can be pulled down to ground level in autumn or early spring and covered with soil, leaving the tips showing; the stems can be planted when they have rooted
History	salvia comes from the Latin *salveo*, to heal, and sage had a tremendous medical reputation from ancient times to the Middle Ages. An English proverb has it that: 'he who would live for aye, Must eat Sage in May'

Sage *plant*

Not only stuffing
Although sage is firmly established as a main ingredient in the stuffing of poultry and game, it has strong therapeutic values, being rich in pinene, cineol and thujone.

Savory

(Culinary) *Satureja spp*

Description	hardy perennials; flowering mid–to late summer; height; *summer savory* 15-20cm (6-8in), *winter savory* 25-45cm (9-18in)
Uses	aromatic leaves are sharp and spice-like in their flavour; use them fresh with broad beans, runners and French beans, also with peas, salads, cucumbers, soups and rich meats
Site/soil	sun and well-drained, fertile soil for summer savory *(S. hortensis)*; sun and poor, dryish soil for winter savory *(S. montana)*
Sow/plant	sow summer savory outdoors in mid spring, and thin to 15cm (6in) apart; plant winter savory where it is to grow in mid spring also, and space at 30cm (12in)
Cultivate	thin summer savory early to prevent it becoming straggly; a shady place will have the same effect on both kinds; winter savory is slower-growing, and hard cutting every spring will form it into a compact dwarf shrub; it roots readily when layered in spring; winter savory is long-lived but cloche it in winter to protect from snow
Harvest	pluck leaves when needed from established plants
History	the ancient Romans thought savory belonged to the Satyrs, hence the name and the fact that it was thought to be an aphrodisiac; savory was one of the garden plants listed in the 12th century by the Abbot of Cirencester

Savory *plant*

Sauces and dressing
Savory, both summer and winter types, is excellent for adding to other highly flavoured preparations. It can be added to many sauces, including horseradish, and steeped in vinegar to be used in French dressings.

Savory *leaf detail*

Skullcap

(Medicinal) *Scutellaria galericulata*

Description	short-lived herbaceous perennial, dies down in autumn, creeping; flowers in mid–late summer; height, flower stems 15-45cm (6-18in)
Uses	Skullcap is thought to have a considerable ameliorative effect on the nerves, nervous headaches, hysteria and a variety of other nervous disorders, and also has good results in the treatment of hydrophobia
Site/soil	sun and any soil, preferably with good drainage
Sow/plant	sow seed outdoors in mid spring in a shaded seed-bed, and transplant in early autumn to its permanent position, spaced 15cm (6in) apart
Cultivate	no particular cultivation is needed, other than to keep the seedlings and young plants free from weeds; the best plants are obtained in poorish, rather than rich soil; increase by digging up in spring, dividing, and replanting the best pieces
Harvest	dig up the whole plant in early summer, and dry
History	the common name for the American species, *S. laterifolia,* is Mad-dog Skullcap or Madweed; the name comes from the Latin *scutella,* a little dish, in reference to one of the outer parts of the flower, which in due course forms a kind of lid on top of the seed capsule; there are several ornamental forms of skullcap, though none has ever gained much popularity

Skullcap *detail*

The madweed
The use of skullcap in the treatment of rabies is probably its only claim to fame, but it can make an attractive border plant if not overshadowed by other plants.

85

Sorrel, French

(Culinary) *Rumex scutatus*

Description	hardy herbaceous perennial, dies down in autumn; flowers early–late summer; height 45-60cm (18-24in)
Uses	chopped up fresh leaves make very good soup; because of their acid flavour use them sparingly in salads, cream cheese and garnishes; French sorrel has the best flavour, but all sorrels contain a good deal of vitamin C
Site/soil	sun or a little shade, any soil, preferably moist
Sow/plant	sow seed outdoors mid spring and thin to 45-60cm (1½-2ft) apart; plant also in mid spring
Cultivate	keep well watered in dry weather and remove flowering stems; mulch with rotted garden compost or similar material in early spring each year; protect in severe cold; increase by division in spring or early autumn
Harvest	take leaves as required, but do not strip young plants; fleshy leaves need careful drying
History	French sorrel is thought to have been introduced to Britain in 1596, when it took the place of garden sorrel because of its more agreeable flavour. The doctors of ancient Rome considered that sorrel had medicinal properties and recommended it for use in kidney complaints; Culpeper advised the use of the leaves 'wrapped in a large colewort leaf and roasted in the embers', for 'ripening and breaking' boils

Sorrel *plant*

On the spot treatment
A poultice made from cooked sorrel is known to bring boils and abscesses rapidly to a head – but it may be the heat of the poultice that does it.

Sweet Cicely

(Culinary) *Myrrhis odorata*

Description	hardy perennial, dies down late autumn, grows again late winter; flowers late spring–early summer; height 75-120cm (2½-4ft)
Uses	aniseed-flavoured leaves can be added to fruit salads, trifles, ice-cream, summer wine cups and fruit drinks, also to salads, soups and herb butter; fruits are sometimes used green, chopped up and mixed with other herbs
Site/soil	a little shade, well-drained, fertile soil
Sow/plant	sow seed outdoors in mid spring in a seed-bed, and transplant to its permanent place when 10 or 13cm (4 or 5in) high, spaced 45-60cm (1½-2ft) apart; seed is slow to germinate
Cultivate	slow to grow, but it has a deep-rooting taproot, and can be difficult to eliminate because of self-sowing; plant in an out-of-the-way part of the garden and remove flowering stems unless seeds are wanted
Harvest	strip fern-like leaves as required after early spring-late autumn; seeds are used, dried, when ripe and brown, and then pulverized
History	once a very popular culinary herb; the leaves were widely used, and eaten as a tonic; the name *myrrhis* is said to derive from the Greek word for perfume, *myrrh;* in the 16th and 17th centuries the crushed seeds were an ingredient of mixtures for polishing and scenting furniture, and they are still one of the ingredients of Chartreuse liqueur

Sweet Cicely *plant*

Sugar substitute

Sweet Cicely is one of the most unusual herbs in that it has a very considerable ability to sweeten dishes in which it is used. A few leaves put into dishes which usually require sugar may reduce the sugar needed by as much as half. It is best used with fruits that tend not to be sweet, such as gooseberries and rhubarb, and it is also good for jams made from mulberries.

Tansy

(Culinary, medicinal) *Tanacetum vulgare*

Description	ornamental, hardy perennial, dying down in autumn; flowers midsummer–early autumn; height 60-90cm (2-3ft)
Uses	fresh young leaves, with their strong and curious odour, or the juice from them, are used for making tansy cake, pudding, fritters and pancakes; tansy tea made from the leaves and flowers is said to be calming, and the leaves pounded together can be applied to sprains for relief of pain and swelling; opinions vary as to whether the plant is poisonous, but tansy leaves cannot be sold in the USA
Site/soil	sun and any soil, preferably on the heavy side
Sow/plant	sow seed outdoors in spring and thin to 30-35cm (12-15in)
Cultivate	tansy grows wild in many places, and no particular cultivation is required; the creeping roots will result in one plant slowly taking up a larger piece of ground than when first planted, and it is easily increased by division in spring and autumn
Harvest	remove leaves as required, flowers just as they open fully
History	tansy remains in flower for many weeks, hence its Greek name *Athanasie,* which means everlasting; it was formerly a strewing herb used for disinfecting churches and courts of law, protecting clothes from moths and keeping flies away from meat; tansy cake, was made at the end of Lent, for Easter

Tansy *plant*

Fly repellent
Tansy leaves when crushed release a volatile oil which flies, fleas and other undesirable insects are unwilling to come near. Unfortunately, the effects fairly soon wear off.

Tarragon, French

(Culinary) *Artemisia dracunculus*

Tarragon *plant*

Description	more or less hardy herbaceous perennial; flowers midsummer but flowers do not open completely and do not set seed; height 60-90cm (2-3ft)
Uses	leaves have an entirely individual, sweetish flavour which is very strong; they are used sparingly with steaks, mushrooms, omelettes and other egg dishes, sauce tartare, grilled fish, and as part of *fines herbes*; sprigs are used for flavouring vinegar
Site/soil	sun, shelter; good soil drainage is very important for winter survival
Sow/plant	plant in late spring at least 60cm (2ft) apart
Cultivate	protect from cold while establishing, and keep free of weeds; tarragon grows best on poorish soil, so does not need feeding; lift and replant every few years to maintain flavour, and increase by division in spring; protect only in severely cold weather
Harvest	strip leaves from early summer–early autumn; dry at blood-heat only and handle leaves carefully, to avoid loss of natural oils
History	the common name is derived from the French word *estragon,* little dragon – it was thought to heal the bites of snakes, serpents, scorpions and so on; a dictionary of 1538 listed tarragon, saying that it 'hath a taste like gynger', and John Evelyn, the 17th century diarist, described it as 'one of the perfuming or spicy furnitures of our sallets'

To make tarragon butter
Cream 100g of butter until it is soft. Add to it 30ml (2 tablespoons) of chopped fresh tarragon and beat together. Add salt, black pepper and a little lemon juice. Shape into rolls and put into the refrigerator to harden. Serve with grilled fish.

Thyme

(Culinary) *Thymus spp*

Description	small, evergreen sub-shrubs, hardy except for lemon thyme; flowers midsummer; height 30cm (1ft) but caraway thyme may be creeping
Uses	leaves of garden thyme *(T. vulgaris)*, fresh or dried, with all meat dishes, sausages, fish, egg dishes, cheeses – especially mixed with cream cheese, and as part of bouquet garni; lemon thyme *(T. x citriodorus)* in custards, milk puddings, fruit salads and the blander fish and meats; the leaves of the caraway thyme *(T. herba barona)* can be substituted for caraway seeds
Site/soil	sun, shelter and a poor, well-drained soil, preferably chalky
Sow/plant	plant in mid–late spring 45cm (1½ft) apart
Cultivate	hot dry conditions produce the best flavoured thyme, and on stony soils it tends to self-seed; no particular care is needed beyond trimming the plants back after flowering to encourage new growth; easily increased by semi-ripe cuttings 5cm (2in) long taken in summer; replace parents every 4 years or so
History	Gerard lists in his Herbal a wild thyme with white flowers 'the white kinde I found at South fleet in Kent' – garden thyme is normally purple-flowered. *Thymus* comes from the Greek word *thuo*, to perfume, and the 17th century essayist Francis Bacon advised that garden walks 'should be set with burnet, wild thyme and water-mints as they perfume the air, being trodden upon and crushed'

Thyme *plant*

The cleansing herb
Thyme was used in very ancient periods of history for embalming the dead and for purifying meat. In recent times it has become clear that the plant contains a very strong antiseptic. The ancient Greeks, Romans and others were right – but how they came to be right about this plant, and wrong about so many others, we shall never know. Thyme comes closer to being a panacea than any other herb, being effective in the treatment of many respiratory and intestinal infections.

Valerian

(Medicinal) *Valeriana officinalis*

Description	hardy perennial, dies down in autumn; flowers midsummer; height 90-120cm (3-4ft)
Uses	mainly as a sedative or tranquillizer for nervous troubles of all kinds; tea made from the unpleasant and strong-smelling roots is calming and soothing
Site/soil	sun or a little shade, most soils, preferably moist fertile ones
Sow/plant	plant in mid spring 60cm (2ft) apart
Cultivate	keep well weeded, and water in dry weather; liquid-feed occasionally while growing, and mulch with rotted garden compost in spring each year; increase from rooted offsets in early autumn
Harvest	dig up roots in late autumn of the second year from planting, wash soil off completely, split up into sections and dry thoroughly; store in really air-tight containers
History	the common name comes from the Latin *valere,* to be healthy, and it previously had a tremendous reputation for its medicinal properties, being thought a cure for everything from epilepsy to insomnia; its other common name *Phu,* is one's instinctive reaction to the smell of the roots which are, surprisingly, as popular with cats as catmint; Valerian was mentioned in the lists of Anglo-Saxon doctors and, much later, Culpeper was advocating its use for 'headaches, trembling, palpitations, vapours and hysteric complaints'

Valerian *plant*

The ratcatcher's herb
During the 18th Century, and even later, ratcatchers used pieces of valerian root as bait for the rats.

Vervain, Holy Herb

(Medicinal) *Verbena officinalis*

Description	hardy herbaceous perennial, dying down in autumn; flowers late in early summer into midsummer; height 30cm (1ft)
Uses	vervain tea, made from the fresh, slightly bitter flavoured leaves used as a nightcap to encourage sleep, and as a digestive, sweetened with honey; also thought to be useful as a nerve tonic, to help in eliminating constant headaches and to clear and improve the eyesight
Site/soil	sun and a fertile, well-drained soil
Sow/plant	sow seed thinly outdoors in early spring, and thin to 30cm (1ft) apart; plant in late spring–early summer at the same spacing
Cultivate	vervain requires no particular cultivation beyond keeping the seedlings free of weeds, and watering in dry weather; increase by division in mid spring
Harvest	strip the leaves or leafy stems from mature plants at any time from late spring, or strip for drying in early summer and avoid bruising as the essential oil is easily lost
History	vervain has strong associations with the Druids and, indeed, was thought to have magical properties; it was used in sacrificial rites and a pendant of the leaves was a good luck charm; the Celtic name *ferfaen* meant to drive away a stone, in reference to its remedial effect on the bladder; although a native European plant, vervain is now widespread in the USA

Vervain *plant and leaf detail*

The sorcerer's herb
At the end of the 16th Century Matthiolus said: 'Sorcerers lose their senses at the mention of this herb. For they say that those who are rubbed with it will obtain all they ask, and that it will cure fevers and cause a person to love another, and ... that it cures all illnesses and more besides.'

Woad

(Cosmetic, medicinal) *Isatis tinctoria*

Description	biennial or short-lived perennial; flowers early–late summer; height 60-90cm (2-3ft)
Uses	the crushed leaves produce a blue colouring substance, no longer used as a dye itself commercially because it has been superseded by indigo; also occasionally used as a styptic for cuts and other wounds
Site/soil	sun or a little shade, fertile soil in good condition
Sow/plant	sow seed in late summer and thin 2 weeks after germination to about 15cm (6in) apart
Cultivate	in the spring after sowing remove overwintered weeds and thereafter keep free of weeds with careful cultivation. Liquid-feed occasionally while growing, especially if the soil is rather poor; replace plants every 3 years or so – it will self-sow
Harvest	cut the leaves as flowering approaches, dry a little, crush to paste and leave exposed to the air but protected from rain until it ferments; when fermentation is complete, after about 2 weeks, mix again, moisten and ferment further; infuse the material finally obtained with limewater to bring out the colour of the dye
History	though woad was thought to have been used as a skin decoration and to dye home-woven cloth, it was probably also used to stop bleeding; *Waad* was the Anglo-Saxon name for it

Woad *plant and leaf detail*

Wearing woad
Whether the ancient inhabitants of Scandinavia and Britain really decorated themselves with woad or whether they merely experimented with it before discovering how to use it as a dye, there is no doubt that it was discovered a very long time ago, and it was worn, in the form of dyed clothing, until very recent times.

Wormwood, Green Ginger

(Medicinal, culinary) *Artemisia absinthium*

Description	hardy perennial, dying down in autumn, flowers midsummer; height 45-60cm (1½-2ft)
Uses	the tops of the shoots and young leaves, infused, act as a digestive and a tonic, and prevent nausea, but should not form a strong infusion; bitter-tasting leaves are also used in small quantities for making Vermouth and in a variety of liqueurs and aperitifs, and as a worm repellent
Site/soil	some shade, and any soil, preferably well-drained
Sow/plant	sow seed in early autumn soon after ripening, and thin to about 60cm (2ft); plant at the same time and same spacing
Cultivate	keep the seedlings free of weeds and weed well after overwintering; increase by dividing in autumn or early spring
Harvest	cut off upper parts of stems when in flower and dry in gentle warmth
History	wormwood was thought to offset poisoning by hemlock and toadstools, and was highly thought of by Hippocrates for improving disorders of the brain; in medieval days it was used throughout Europe as a deterrent for body lice, the bug and the flea and it is still recommended as a vermifuge; William Tusser, a gardening writer of 1573, wrote: 'While wormwood hath seed get a handful or twain, to save against March, to make flea to refraine'

Wormwood *plant*

Absinthe

Wormwood was the principal ingredient of the infamous liqueur which caused so much harm in 19th Century France. Its destructive effects upon the brain have been equalled or exceeded only by the more obnoxious narcotics. And yet wormwood is a fairly inoffensive plant, more beneficial than harmful. It is very effective as a diuretic and as an aid to digestion. Repeated use, however, may irritate the gastric mucosa.

Index

Acknowledgments

The 'How To' Book of Herbs and
Herb Gardening was created by
Simon Jennings and Company Limited.
We are grateful to the following
individuals and organisations
for their assistance in the
making of this book:

Hazel Breeden: *picture research*
John Couzins: *cover and title page photographs*
The Dover Archive: *engravings and embellishments*
Ann Hall: *compilation of index*
Anthony Huxley: *additional research*
Marta Jennings: *additional artwork*
Carole Johnson: *line and tone illustrations*
Susan Milne: *colour illustrations*
Coral Mula: *line and tone illustrations*
Chris Perry: *hand tinting of engravings*

Photographs
Pat Brindley: pages **6** *tl, tr, c,* **7** *tr, c,* **22** *tl,* **26** *tl*
Mary Evans Picture Library: page **22** *bl*
The Mansell Collection: page **7** *l*
British Museum, London: pages **11, 23**
Harry Smith Horticultural Collection: pages **7** *tl,* **10** *tl, bl,* **26** *bl, c,* **27**

abbreviations: *c* centre; *tl* top left; *tr* top right; *bl* bottom left; *l* left

Typesetting by Text Filmsetters Ltd., Orpington, Kent
Headline setting by Diagraphic Typesetting Ltd., London
Additional display setting by Facet Photosetting, London

Special thanks to Norman Ruffell and
the staff of Swaingrove Ltd., Bury St. Edmunds,
Suffolk, for the lithographic reproduction.